LOGICAL
THINKING

LOGICAL THINKING

RICHARD L. PURTILL
Western Washington State College

Harper & Row, Publishers
New York, Evanston, San Francisco, London

*Most people don't think that the proper use of infer-
ences and hypotheses and questioning, and logic in
general, has any relation to what we have to do in life.
Now in every kind of action the question is how a wise
and good man can come out of it with integrity. So we
must either say that a wise man won't bother with
difficult problems, or won't deal with them thoroughly
if he does, or else we must admit that he ought to learn
the way to solve these problems. For what is reasoning?
Accepting the truth, rejecting falsehood, suspending
judgment in doubtful cases. Is it enough just to know
this? If you say it is, ask yourself if it would be enough
just to know that counterfeit money exists. You must
admit that it wouldn't be, that you should be able to
tell good money from bad. In the same way, in reasoning we should be able to give proofs and distinguish
between the true, the false, and the doubtful—that much
is clear.*

Epictetus, Discourses *Book I, Chapter 7*

CONTENTS

TO THE
INSTRUCTOR

Almost everyone would agree that a course in logical
thinking might be good for most college students, but
not everyone would agree what ought to be taught
in such a course. Symbolic logic, traditional Aristotelian
logic, the study of fallacies, and many other topics all
have some claim to consideration. None of them,
however, seems to be the one thing necessary.
Apparently a combination of topics is indicated. But
with too many topics, the course is overloaded or
else consists merely of snippets from this and that.

In planning this book I asked myself two questions.
First, what is the essential minimum of logic that any
well-educated person ought to be familiar with?
Second, how much logic is the student likely to
retain and use some time after having taken the course?
A realistic answer to the second question helped me
to moderate my expectations about an answer to the
first. Ideally, the educated man should know more
about logic than this book will tell him, but in
practice he is likely to remember only what he can
use. A person who wants to think more clearly and
critically will, I hope, find everything in this book
useful for that purpose. If his curiosity is aroused and
he wants to know more about logic, there are

several excellent books (some of which I list in the bibliography) to take him on to the next stage.

You will find that I have treated most of the traditional topics: definition and classification, informal fallacies, deductive and inductive reasoning. But I have also added some topics not usually dealt with in this kind of book—a chapter on organization, for example—and I have tried to bring a fresh approach to some of the usual topics. In my treatment of deductive and inductive reasoning I have done my best to reduce these subjects to their essentials, hoping that the essentials will be remembered and used.

I made my examples and exercises as lively and contemporary as possible, but they are necessarily limited. I urge you to make your own collection of examples from current books, magazines, and newspapers, and where practical from movies, television, and radio. One useful kind of supplementary assignment for students is to ask them to find such examples.

Very few of the exercises in the book can be graded in a mechanical fashion, and since you will probably not be able to make detailed comments on every paper you may find it useful to take class time in going over some good answers and some poor answers to the exercises you assign. Students are often excellent critics of other students' answers, and you might make use of reproducing devices, overhead projectors, etc., to give them a chance to criticize.

Some teachers trained in logic may feel there is too little formal logic in this book, and some teachers without this training may feel there is too much. I urge the logicians to consider the kind of class they are teaching and ask themselves whether their students are as interested in logic as they themselves are. The other group is not so easy to answer. I hope that this book will be used in classes taught in English and speech departments as well as philosophy, and that it will serve as a supplement in courses where it is not the main text. In such courses the time spent on logic may have to be limited, but there is a certain minimum that must be taught if you are really going

to teach logic and not just pretend to. This book comes
fairly close to that minimum, though some of it
might be skipped if the topic is treated another way
and a good deal of it can be left to the student to read
on his own.

I would like to thank the research office at Western
Washington State College for help in preparing the
manuscript of this book, and Mrs. Anne Drake for
typing it. I would also like to thank John Ryden and
Jim Martin of Harper & Row.

This book is based on a course I have taught for
a number of years and which many students have told
me they found enjoyable and useful. Relevance is,
after all, a logician's concept, and I hope that this book
will help you show your students that no matter what
our problems may be, clear and critical thinking
is always relevant.

**LOGICAL
THINKING**

INTRODUCTION

Will a logic book help you to think more clearly, more critically, and more responsibly? It depends both on you and on the book. If you habitually think with your emotions, jump to conclusions, and follow your prejudices without ever questioning them, and if you have no intention of changing your ways, then probably no logic book on earth will be of much help to you. But even if you are aware of shortcomings in your thinking and really want to do something about thinking more logically, there are a great many logic books that may give you no help. For example, a book on symbolic logic written for mathematicians who are interested in studying logic as a mathematical system is not likely to be of much direct use in improving your reasoning in everyday situations.

This book is written as a sort of "how to" book to help you think more logically in ordinary circumstances. Just as a book on carpentry for the home handyman is not written for the man who plans to become a professional carpenter, this book is not written for the person who plans to become a philosopher or mathematician. A good "how to" book will explain a good many things that seem obvious to the professional, and leave out a great many things which seem important to the professional mind. But if such a book helps someone to do some things he couldn't do before, it is a success. A good book of this kind also helps the beginner to see when a job is too hard for him and when he needs an expert.

It may happen that someone who starts out to build a doghouse by reading a "how to" book finds eventually that he is good at carpentry and enjoys doing it. He may even decide to become a professional carpenter. Perhaps some of you who are reading this book may find that logic is fascinating, that you do it well and enjoy it. You may want to go on to other books, the kind that are written for philosophers or mathematicians to help them do the sort of difficult reasoning needed in their own fields. Toward the end of this book, I tell you a little about such uses of logic and recommend some further reading. But most of the book is on a more practical level.

As a philosopher and logician, I have taught a number of introductory courses in logic, philosophy, and sometimes even mathematics. One course I have taught on and off for years is an introductory logic course that covers about the same material as this book. An interesting fact about this course is that older people —mostly secretaries working for the college who were taking a few courses on the side—often did better on the average than the freshmen and sophomores who made up most of the class. Now there could be all sorts of explanations for this. But I think that one possible explanation is that these people, who had lived somewhat longer and perhaps faced more problems and overcome more difficulties than the average student, had already been forced to pick up some of what I was trying to teach in the course about thinking and problem solving. At least in some cases, the older the wiser. If this book can make you a bit wiser before you are too much older, it will be a success.

This book can be used in two ways. First, it may be used as a textbook in a course like the one I have just described, and if so I would urge the teacher to spend a fair amount of time talking about actual examples taken from newspapers, magazines, radio, television, etc. The book presents a number of rules, principles, and techniques that will make much more sense when applied to actual cases than if they are merely discussed in the abstract. Second, the book can be used by a person simply reading it on his own, without taking a course in logic. This person may be a student to whom the book has been assigned as supplementary reading, or someone not in school who is interested in improving his reasoning. I would urge these people also to apply what they read to actual situations. You wouldn't read a book on photography without meaning to take some pictures, so don't read this book without applying it.

As you will see from the table of contents, this book is divided into three main sections: analysis, criticism, and argument. These divisions correspond to three important characteristics of logical thinking: clarity, awareness of difficulties, and the responsible basing of decisions on evidence. Three important aids to clear thinking are: definition, which helps us know what our words mean; classification, which helps us sort out our data; and organization, which enables us to attack a problem without wasted effort. Three important difficulties we need to be aware of in reasoning are the assumptions that we so often bring with us to a problem, the fallacious arguments that can mislead or betray us, and the weak arguments that we tend to rely on too much. Finally, in order to arrive at responsible decisions on the basis of the evidence, we have to know something of what logicians have discovered about the two main kinds of reasoning, deduction and induction.

After each section you will find cases to which you may apply the principles just discussed. Some of these are imaginary, some real. The later ones tend to be more complex than the earlier ones, but most of them do not have simple clear-cut solutions. Very few real-life problems do.

PART ONE
ANALYSIS

In this section we consider three ways of clarifying our thinking: definition, classification, and organization. Definition helps us avoid disputes that are really about words although they seem to be about matters of substance. Definition also helps us to avoid ambiguity and vagueness, and to be sure that we are using words with a precise meaning. Classification enables us to deal with the confusing variety of the world around us by grouping together things that have similar characteristics. Organization enables us to deal with complex material in a clear and orderly fashion. Mastery of the techniques of definition, classification, and organization should enable you to avoid confusion and attack problems in a sensible and efficient manner.

CHAPTER 1
DEFINITION

ARGUMENTS ABOUT WORDS

Often a dispute cannot be resolved because the opposing parties are using a term in two different ways without either of them quite recognizing it. We will call such cases verbal disputes. Imagine a dispute at Western University between Frederick X of the Black Students Union and Dean Wood, the academic dean. Frederick X angrily claims that Western University is a racist institution, while Dean Wood hotly denies it. If we look carefully at the statements made by these two gentlemen we find that Frederick X and the BSU mean by *racist institution* any institution that in fact discriminates against minority races, whatever the intention, while Dean Wood and his colleagues mean by *racist institution* any institution that *intentionally* discriminates against minority races. In effect Frederick X is saying "Western U has policies that are in fact unfair to minority races," while Dean Wood is saying "Western U does not intend to discriminate against any minority race." Both may *know* they are right; Frederick X has evidence that Western U's admission tests are biased in favor of middle-class white values and experiences, and Dean Wood has evidence that the faculty and administration of Western U are very much concerned with justice for minority races.

In this somewhat idealized situation, once Frederick X and Dean Wood realize they mean different things by *racist institution* it is at least possible that they may be able to cooperate. But so long as Dean Wood thinks Frederick X is accusing him of intentional discrimination and Frederick X thinks Dean Wood is trying to deny the actual bias of Western U's admission policies, they are unlikely to even begin to cooperate.

If Frederick X and Dean Wood begin by asking "What do you mean by saying a certain institution is racist?" or "What evidence would show that an institution is or is not racist?" they still might quarrel about it. But at least they are no longer arguing at cross-purposes. It may seem unrealistic to expect opposing parties to begin by carefully defining terms and making sure they clearly understand the key terms. But it is even more unrealistic to expect disputes to be settled when the disputants mean different things by the key terms being used.

Of course even when this source of disagreement is removed, there may be many other differences about facts or values that make agreement impossible. Frederick X may claim that requiring knowledge of Shakespeare's plays on the entrance exam at Western U shows a bias in favor of white culture, and Dean Wood may deny this. Dean Wood may try to refute the claim of racism by showing that many of his faculty have been involved in civil rights activities, and Frederick X may dismiss such activities as tokenism. Again, it may be possible to clarify some terms in an effort to reach agreement: "What constitutes a bias in favor of white culture? How much effort or sacrifice must be expended before a commitment to a cause can no longer be dismissed as tokenism?" There may very well be differences of value that are seemingly unreconcilable and differences about facts that are difficult to settle, but if it is *recognized* that there are differences about matters of fact, they can, in principle, be settled. Differences in values are not so easy to reconcile, but if they are clearly recognized, negotiation or compromise may become possible.

To begin to draw some specific morals from our

story: First we must notice that in any given dispute there are likely to be only a few key terms about which misunderstanding is likely to lead to argument at cross-purposes. Dean Wood and Frederick X understood well enough what they meant by *institution, minority race, entrance exam,* and so on. So the first thing to do is isolate the terms that may be causing trouble. The second is to try to see if these key terms are being used in different ways by the two parties to the dispute. If so, a brief explanation, not necessarily a formal definition, should be given of what each party means by this term. Finally, it may be helpful to take some steps to avoid further arguing at cross-purposes. Perhaps Frederick X and Dean Wood could agree that racism in the sense meant by Frederick X could be called unconscious racism and in the sense meant by Dean Wood, conscious racism. The dispute might then be put in these terms: "Granted that Western U is not a consciously racist institution, is it nevertheless an unconsciously racist institution?" It might be well also to avoid further confusion by clarifying what is meant by *unconscious racism,* and seeing if agreement can be reached on what constitutes evidence that an institution is unconsciously racist.

We can summarize the lessons we have learned from this example of a verbal dispute as follows:

1. Try to isolate the key term or terms that are being used differently by the disputants.
2. Give a brief explanation of the different ways the term is being understood by each side.
3. Try to avoid further confusion by using new or modified terminology and by trying to agree on standards of evidence.

AMBIGUITY AND VAGUENESS

In verbal disputes like the one we have just discussed, presumably each party knows what *he* means by the key terms; the problem is that each of the other parties means something different. In other cases, however, arguments or confusion may arise because of the vagueness or ambiguity of a key term. Ordinarily, *vague* and *ambiguous* are used interchangeably, but we will use these terms in a special way. By a vague term we will mean a term with *too little* meaning, by an ambiguous term we will mean a term with *too much* meaning.

How can a term have too little meaning? Consider a word such as *nice*. When people talk about "a nice day," "a nice boy," "a nice dinner," and so on, the word has so little meaning that it says almost nothing. Perhaps some vague general approval is usually implied, but even this cannot be counted on. For example people say "It was a nice enough dinner, but I didn't like it" or "He was a nice boy, but who likes nice boys?" Of course it is often possible to guess what the speaker means by *nice day* or a *nice boy* if you know the speaker or the circumstances. A nice day for Sam may be a good surfing day, while a nice day for Sally may be a good skiing day. A boy who is described by Susan's mother as a nice boy might be described by Susan as wishy-washy. The point is that you do have to guess, you do have to know the speaker or the circumstances. The word itself tells you very little.

On the other hand, a word that does not mean too little may mean too much. That is, it may have a number of possible meanings. Each of these meanings may be specific enough but which specific meaning is intended may be unclear. If a word has just two possible meanings and it is unclear which one is meant, it is called an *equivocal* term. If a word has two or more possible meanings and we are not sure which one is meant, we will say that the word is *ambiguous*. Consider, for example, the word *simple* as used in the phrase *a simple meal*. As C. S. Lewis points out in his book *Studies in Words*[1] a simple meal can be a meal which is

1. Easy to prepare, or
2. Plain, not fancy, expensive, or elaborate, or
3. Made of only a few ingredients—not a mixture of different things.

A meal of caviar and crackers is simple in senses 1 and 3, but not in sense 2, while a casserole of left-

[1]Cambridge University Press, New York, 1967, p. 175.

overs may be simple in sense 2, but not in sense 3, and may or may not be simple in sense 1.

Are vagueness and ambiguity always undesirable? This depends a good deal on what you are trying to accomplish. To describe a day as warm is comparatively vague, yet for some purposes it is sufficiently precise. In casual conversation about the weather we can say "It's a warm day" rather than "The temperature is sixty-two degrees in the sun and fifty-eight degrees in the shade." But if I am wondering whether to wear a topcoat for a walk, take just a jacket, or go in shirtsleeves, the information that the day is warm is not precise enough to give me much information. Similarly in a story about mountain climbing "They had a simple meal and then began the ascent" may be precise enough, but to a cook, the order "Cook me a simple meal" would be much too imprecise.

Often the context or our background knowledge removes vagueness or ambiguity. If one skier says to another as they go up the lift "It's going to be a nice day," presumably he means a good skiing day. If I say to my wife "You've had a hard day, dear, cook a simple meal," then by *simple* I obviously mean easy to prepare.

One way of avoiding vagueness and ambiguity is to define terms, as we will see shortly. But we can often avoid confusion or misunderstanding by simply being as precise as the situation requires. If my wife is going out to garden and asks me "What's it like out?" it would be more helpful of me to say "Warm enough to go without a coat, if you stay in the sun" than simply to say "warm." Or rather than ask my wife to cook a simple meal for a visiting relative, I would be more helpful to say "Cook something simple for Aunt Minnie; she won't eat much and she doesn't like fancy cooking anyway." Here I am advising her to cook a meal that is simple in two senses: easy to prepare and plain.

In some social situations vagueness may be desirable. If someone who has no business knowing asks why George was fired, we may prefer to say vaguely "He just didn't work out" rather than explain precisely "He drank like a fish and stole everything that wasn't nailed down." In poetic and other evocative uses of language we may deliberately use a word in an ambiguous way, playing on its many meanings. But for ordinary descriptive discourse both vagueness and ambiguity should be avoided. To strike a personal note, many student themes could be improved if the student asked himself "Would I understand this if I were the teacher?"

ANALYTIC DEFINITION

One way of avoiding both verbal disputes and vagueness or ambiguity is to define key terms so that everyone will be sure to understand them and interpret them the same way. In some definitions we simply announce that we are going to use a word in a certain way, for example "For the purposes of this study *executive* shall mean a person who supervises the work of at least one other employee." Such definitions are called *stipulative* definitions. In stipulative definitions we are generally not concerned with whether or not the definition agrees with the way people ordinarily use the term. One danger of giving stipulative definitions of terms in ordinary use is that we tend to forget our stipulation and slip into using the word in the ordinary way. A psychologist may stipulate that by *intelligence* he means only what can be measured by certain tests, then slip into saying something like "Of course we want only the more intelligent high school students to go to college." This may be true if the ordinary sense of *intelligent* is meant. But if we use *intelligent* in the psychologist's stipulative sense, what is meant is that we want only the students who do well on these tests to go on to college. Unless these tests are superior to most present ones they probably omit certain factors important to intelligence in the usual sense, such as creativity, and are likely to be unfair to certain social groups. Thus we may disagree that only students who do well on these tests should go to college.

Another kind of definition, which we will somewhat unfairly call *dictionary definition*, consists of simply using a synonym for a troublesome word, for example, defining the adjective *racist* as *discriminatory*. This sort of definition may be useful where the synonym is more familiar than the term being defined, but it is unlikely to solve the problems that arise in connection with verbal disputes or in connection with vagueness or ambiguity. Substituting *discriminatory* for *racist* in our example of a verbal dispute still leaves it unclear whether conscious or unconscious discrimination is meant. Substituting *plain* for *simple* may be some help in making *simple meal* less ambiguous, but is not an adequate solution because *plain* also has several senses, though perhaps not quite as many as *simple*. In fact, only very short or very inadequate dictionaries rely heavily on what we call dictionary definitions, and such dictionaries are rarely helpful in avoiding confusions about words.

The sort of definition that is likely to be helpful in avoiding confusion about words is what we will call *analytic definition*. In giving an analytic definition we try to give a *clear and general account of the way in which a word is used*. The account must be *clear* because our main purpose is to avoid confusion due to misunderstandings about words. But it must also be *general*. I might give a *clear* idea of what the simple meal was that the mountaineers had in our earlier example by saying that in this case the simple meal consisted of crackers, beef jerky, tea, and chocolate. But this is not a *general* account; not all simple meals consist of crackers, beef jerky, etc. Mathematics gives us easy examples of clear and general definitions. For example, we define a triangle as a closed figure with three straight sides, and an even number as a number divisible by 2 without remainder. These definitions are clear and they are general; that is, they apply to everything we ordinarily call a triangle or an even number.

Notice that as opposed to stipulative definitions, analytic definitions are accounts of *the way in which a word is used*. Thus if you can show that an analytic definition does not in fact give a correct account of the way in which a word is used, you have shown that it is not a good analytic definition. If you define a block as a rectangular piece of wood, your definition is defective, for there are plastic blocks, metal blocks, etc.

One way of seeing whether a proposed analytic definition is satisfactory is to check it against certain traditional rules of definition that are direct consequences of our aims in giving analytic definitions. These rules can be stated as follows:

1. A definition should not be obscure or metaphorical.
2. A definition should not be negative where it could be positive.
3. A definition should not be circular.
4. A definition should not be too broad.
5. A definition should not be too narrow.
6. A definition should state an important characteristic of the thing defined.

We will briefly discuss each of these rules and give examples of their application.

1. A definition should not be obscure or metaphorical.
Obviously an obscure definition will not give a *clear* account of the way a word is used. But obscurity can arise in a variety of ways. A technical definition perfectly clear to someone familiar with a certain field may be hopelessly obscure to the uninitiated. Thus in a physics book we might find that a statocoulomb is defined as that charge which if placed 1 cm distant from a charge of the same magnitude and sign will repel the latter with an electrostatic force of 1 dyne. This definition is clear and precise to someone familiar with physics or electronics, but quite obscure to someone who does not know the meaning of the terms *dyne, electrostatic force*, etc. We can see that obscurity is to some extent relative.

Metaphorical definitions, for example Oscar Wilde's definition of a cynic as a man who knows the price of everything and the value of nothing, are often enlightening or funny if we already know what the word means. But they are not likely to clear up confusion or prevent verbal disputes. Thus it is better to avoid them when we are attempting to give an analytic definition of a word.

2. A definition should not be negative where it could be positive.

Some words are almost impossible to define without using negative terms—*orphan* and *bald* are often given as examples. But, in general, explaining what a word does *not* mean is rarely much help in saying what it does mean. Defining *radio* as wireless communication is not very likely to enlighten someone who does not already have some idea of how radio works. Furthermore, negative definitions often leave too many possibilities open—semaphoring with flags is wireless communication, but it is not radio.

3. A definition should not be circular.

A circular definition is one in which a term is sooner or later defined in terms of itself. Obvious cases of circular definition are merely comic. For example in *Hamlet* when Polonius says "to define true madness, why 'tis nothing else but to be mad," we smile at his foolishness. Yet we might be taken in by a pair of definitions such as "cause: what brings about an effect" and "effect: what is brought about by a cause" if we did not see them together. Because the circle is larger, it is not so obvious; but we can see that to know what is meant by *cause* we must know what an effect is, and to know what is meant by *effect* we must know what a cause is. In these definitions cause is really being defined in terms of itself.

Very often definitions given in dictionaries go in a larger or smaller circle. This is usually not a fatal defect in a dictionary, since we often have some idea of what a word means before we look it up, and by going round the circle we see its relation to other similar words and thus get a better idea of what it means. But confusion or verbal disputes are not likely to be cleared up by circular definitions.

Suppose, for example, that a verbal dispute arises about courage when a man rushes into a burning building to save a valuable book. Sam believes this is a courageous act; Sally disagrees, she thinks it is foolish, not courageous. "Let's settle this," says Sam. "Let's look in the dictionary." Sam finds *courageous* defined as having or showing courage, *courage* defined as bravery, and *bravery* defined as being courageous. Obviously these definitions are not much help in settling the verbal dispute or clarifying the idea of courage.

4. A definition should not be too broad.

A definition is too broad if it applies to more things than the word it defines is normally applied to. Thus if we define *automobile* as a self-propelled vehicle, our definition is much too broad. A motorcycle is a self-propelled vehicle, but it is not an automobile. A definition that is too broad may be perfectly clear, positive, and noncircular, but it fails to be a clear and general account *of the way in which a word is used.*

5. A definition should not be too narrow.

A definition that is too narrow applies to fewer things than does the term that is being defined. If I define *automobile* as a four-wheeled self-propelled vehicle with an engine in front, I leave out Volkswagens, which are certainly ordinarily called automobiles. A definition that is too narrow fails to show how a word is used just as much as one that is too broad does.

Some definitions are both too broad and too narrow. If I define *automobile* as a four-wheeled vehicle propelled by an engine, meant for traveling on streets and roads, I leave out such vehicles as jeeps and let in such things as parade floats, which are not automobiles.

6. A definition should state an important characteristic of the thing defined.

Sometimes a definition may state a characteristic that more or less accidentally singles out the same cases as the word defined, but gives us no real insight into the meaning of the term. The story is told that the philosophers of Plato's Academy defined *man* as the featherless biped. The cynic philosopher, Diogenes, feeling that this definition did little justice to human dignity, plucked a live chicken and threw it over the wall of the Academy, shouting "There's your man for you!"

Since importance is often difficult to judge, there may be disputes about what is an important characteristic. If we define *man* as the tool-using animal does this violate rule 6 or not? It might be argued that tool-using is a consequence of more important characteristics, such as intelligence, and that tool-using itself is not decisive. Even if chimpanzees sometimes used tools, we would not on this account say they had become human. However, if certain apes began showing intelligence as great as that of a 5-year-old child, a 6-year-old, and so on, we might say that these apes were evolving into men.

We can see, then, that by an important characteristic we mean the characteristic that makes a difference, a characteristic whose presence or absence decides whether a thing is the sort of thing it is. In this sense, obviously, three-sidedness is an important characteristic of triangles, divisibility by 2 an important characteristic of even numbers, etc. There may be only one such important or *essential* characteristic or there may be more than one.

Merely applying the rules we have just discussed does not show us how to give a good definition, but it does give us standards for judging bad definitions and perhaps gives us some guidelines for making a good definition. Very likely, inventing a really satisfactory definition, like other forms of creativity, needs a certain flair that some people have to a greater extent than others. But anyone can use the rules to criticize a definition already made.

When should we define our terms? The best answer we can give is that we should go to the trouble of defining key terms whenever not defining them would probably cause greater trouble. If there is a real possibility of confusion, or of wasting time on verbal disputes, the time spent on finding and testing definitions for key terms is well spent.

CASES

Try to give a definition of each of the following terms. If you think the term is vague or ambiguous give your reasons. Construct a brief dialogue showing how the term could be the cause of a verbal dispute.

1. rock music
2. drug culture
3. youth culture
4. psychedelic art
5. hippie
6. militant
7. radical
8. liberated woman
9. rap session
10. revolutionary
11. swinger
12. sexism
13. relevance
14. generation gap
15. establishment

Here are some attempts to define terms having to do with emotions. Criticize each definition in terms of the six rules for analytic definitions. (Source: Spinoza, *Ethics*)

16. Envy is hatred insofar as it induces a person to be pained by another's good fortune and to rejoice in another's evil fortune.

17. Empathy is love insofar as it induces a man to feel pleasure at another's good fortune and pain at his misfortune.

18. Self-esteem is pleasure arising from a man's contemplation of himself and his own power of action.

19. Humility is pain arising from a man's contemplation of his own weakness of body and mind.

20. Repentance is pain accompanied by the idea of some action we believe we have performed by the free decision of our mind.

21. Pride is thinking too highly of oneself, from self-love.

22. Honor is pleasure accompanied by the idea of some action of our own, which we believe to be praised by others.

23. Shame is pain accompanied by the idea of some

action of our own which we believe to be blamed by others.

24. Regret is the desire to possess something kept alive by the remembrance of that thing, and at the same time held in check by the thought of other things which prevent us from possessing it.

25. Gratitude is the desire to benefit one who has conferred a benefit on us.

26. Anger is the desire to injure someone whom we hate.

27. Cruelty is the desire to injure someone whom we love or pity.

28. Timidity is the desire to avoid a greater evil, which we dread, by undergoing a lesser evil.

29. Daring is the desire which sets us on to do something our peers are afraid to do.

30. Cowardice is a fear which prevents us from risking some danger which our peers dare to meet.

31. Courtesy is the desire to act in a way which will please others, and to refrain from actions which will displease them.

Some political, philosophical, or religious arguments may be verbal disputes, at least in part. Give an example of such a case from your own experience or reading. Try to find the key term or terms and discuss the different ways in which the term is being understood by each side in the dispute.

CHAPTER 2
CLASSIFICATION

PURPOSES

The basic purpose of classification is simply to let us deal with the world around us. If we made no classifications at all, every individual thing would have to be treated as absolutely unique. This would be tremendously confusing. For example, if early man had not classified one small fuzzy beast together with another as good to eat, harmless, and so on, and large furry beasts, one with another, as dangerous, liable to eat man, and so on, he could hardly have lived long.

Language itself involves classifying things together and referring to them by the same word. As J. R. R. Tolkien says in his essay, "On Fairy-stories":

> The human mind, endowed with the power of generalization and abstraction, sees not only greengrass, discriminating it from other things (and finding it fair to look upon), but sees that it is green as well as being grass. But how powerful, how stimulating to the very faculty that produced it, was the invention of the adjective; no spell or incantation in Faërie is more potent.[1]

[1] *The Tolkien Reader*, Ballantine, New York, 1966, p. 22.

When we call something green, we classify it with
other green things; when we call an animal a dog we
classify it with other dogs. This is classification in the
very widest sense. In the more restricted sense we
classify when we are faced with a group of particular
things and we divide them into groups for some purpose. The librarian classifies books, the farmer classifies eggs or apples, the teacher classifies students in
various ways.

Some of these sorts of classification involve dividing things into groups without making any judgment
about which group is better or worse. The librarian
does not classify books as good or bad, but as fiction or
nonfiction, adult or children's, and so on. Other kinds
of classification do involve a value judgment: Grade AA
eggs sell for more than "checks," well-shaped, unblem-
ished apples are more expensive than deformed or
worm-eaten ones. The teacher may classify students
in both ways: alphabetically when he draws up a class
list, by achievement when he gives grades.

We will call the first sort of classification, where no
element of better or worse is involved, *sorting*, and the
second kind, where evaluation is involved, *grading*. The
ordinary use of the words *sorting* and *grading* suggests
this technical use of the terms, but we will keep the
distinction more strictly than ordinary usage does. It is
always a good idea, when classifying, to ask yourself
"Am I grading or only sorting?"

Any time we classify something, whether we are
sorting or grading, we need certain things. First, we
must have things to classify. If most of us were asked
to classify all the different sorts of people we have
killed, we wouldn't be able to do it because we would
lack any raw material for classification. Second, these
things must be different from each other in some way.
If you give me a hundred identical metal washers and
ask me to classify them, how can I carry out your
request? They are all alike, so there is no way to put
them into classes or groups except arbitrarily. Simply
putting things into arbitrary groups is not classifying
them as I am using the term. We will call putting
things into arbitrary groups *division*. I can *divide* a

hundred identical washers, but I cannot classify them. Third, the things to be classified must be *alike* in some ways. If I had a hundred absolutely unique things, I could not classify them except by putting each one in a unique class, and what would be the point of that? Fortunately, we rarely find two things that have *nothing* whatever in common. With a little ingenuity we can come up with some kind of classification of almost any set of nonidentical things.

But there is no point in classifying just for the sake of classifying. We usually have a purpose in classifying, and this gives us our fourth requirement for classification: a rule or principle telling us what classes the individual things can be sorted into.

For example, suppose that you have given me a handful of coins and told me to sort them out. I sort out the pennies, nickels, dimes, and quarters (finding no fifty-cent pieces). You come back and tell me that you wanted the coins sorted by date and mint, rather than by denomination. Fine, but you should have said so in the first place! The request to sort the coins means nothing unless you tell me what to sort them *into*. What classes you want individuals sorted into depends on your purposes.

What specific purposes do we have for classification? A bewilderingly large number. When I get dressed in the morning I sort my belongings (wallet, keys, change, etc.) by the pocket in which I normally carry them. Here the sorting is a physical operation. I pick up my wallet and put in into one pocket, pick up my change and put it into another pocket. But as I do this I may be mentally sorting out various things I have to do or want to do that day—go to classes, play tennis, stop at the library. I may also grade these occupations: Getting to class is most important, playing tennis next most important (because I've promised a friend), and so on. Or I may sort my activities according to the time they need to be done or physical location—the tennis court may be near the library or near the college. I may need a book before class, or want to stop at the library after tennis because it's on my way home, and so on. But *how* I classify these activities will depend on my purposes, wants, and needs.

We can sum up our results so far as follows:

Classification is a process by which we mentally or physically put together in a group individuals that have some characteristics in common but are not identical, using a rule or principle that tells us what things go into what group.

Sorting is classification where no element of valuation or preference is present.

Grading is classification where some element of valuation or preference *is* present.

Division is putting things into arbitrary groups.

The *general* purpose of classification is to enable us to deal with the world around us in a way that would be impossible if our world consisted of totally unique individuals. The special purposes of classification are as various as life itself.

PRACTICE

Suppose now that we have the raw material for classification, and a purpose for classifying the material. How do we go about making the classification? There are certain very general requirements that apply to any job of classification. We can list them as follows:

1. The classification must be exhaustive; that is, every individual thing to be classified must be put into some class.
2. The classification must be *exclusive;* that is, no individual thing can be put into *more* than one class.
3. The classification must be *clear;* that is, there must be no doubt about which class the individuals should be put into.

These might be called the *logical* requirements for classification. The empirical or practical requirement for classification is that:

4. The classification must be *adequate* for the purpose for which it is intended.

A scheme of classification can meet the first three

requirements, the logical requirements for classification, and yet be unsatisfactory because it fails to meet the fourth requirement. But a scheme of classification that does not meet one or more of the first three requirements is very unlikely to meet the fourth requirement.

Take a case where you are faced with a practical problem in classification. You have to clear an area of ground covered with trees and undergrowth in order to build a summer cabin. The cabin is some distance from any town; in order to bring the proper tools for the job you have to classify the various sorts of vegetation to be cleared. You glance around quickly, see trees and weeds, and on your next trip bring out a scythe for the weeds and an axe for the trees. But when you get to work you find many thick vines and small saplings. They are too tough for your scythe, and cutting them with your axe would take much too much time. Your classification was not *exhaustive*.

Next weekend you come out with a group of friends, determined to get the job done. You decide that a division of labor will be most efficient: You will attack the larger trees with an axe, Tom will get the saplings with a saw, Dick will cut everything under waist-high with a brush-hook, Harry will get the grass and weeds with the scythe. To spur them on, you promise a prize to the one who gets the most done. But very soon Tom and Dick are getting in each other's way. Some saplings are under waist-high, some stuff under waist-high consists of saplings. Your classification was not *exclusive*. Just when you get this settled you find Harry conscientiously cutting a big patch of grass only 4 or 5 inches high, which would have been no obstacle to construction. You wanted only the high grass and weeds cut, but your classification was not *clear* about this.

We can see that in this case a little attention to the logical requirements of classification would have saved you a lot of trouble.

It is harder to give a simple illustration of the dangers of failing to meet the fourth requirement, simply because there are so many ways in which even a clear, exclusive, exhaustive classification can fail to be adequate for its purpose. Remember the case where we imagined you dividing a heap of coins into pennies, nickels, dimes, and quarters. This classification was clear, exclusive, and exhaustive, but since the owner of the coins was interested in them as a coin collector, it was not adequate for his purposes. Or suppose that you are sorting clothes donated for flood victims. You divide them into trousers, shirts, skirts, dresses, under-clothes, and sox. This is a clear, exclusive classification, and let us suppose that for the clothes you have it is exhaustive. But it may lead to all sorts of confusion when the clothing is distributed. Dividing the clothing into adult-size clothing and children's clothing and into male and female clothing in each category might have been a good move. Then if you had time you might sort the clothing by size, separate underclothing and outer clothing, etc.

As this example suggests, one frequently useful move in classification is to try to find large classes that are important ones in relation to your purposes, then sub-divide these classes. Consider, for example, how cloth-ing is usually classified in a large department store. There are men's clothing, women's clothing, and chil-dren's clothing departments. Within the men's depart-ment we find separate areas for suits, slacks, dress and sport shirts, work clothes, underwear, sox, belts, ties, etc. But there will be no skirts, pantyhose, or brassieres. The women's department will have these items but lack some that the men's department has, and the children's department will differ from both. The classification is based on convenience for the store and the shopper, and may change to meet various requirements. For example, there may be a sale table with various kinds of clothing, or a swimsuit section at some seasons but not others.

There is no rule for making a good classification. Some people seem to have more talent for classification than others. But most of us can improve our skill by keeping in mind the logical requirements for classifica-tion and by making an effort to see that our classifica-tions are well thought out in relation to our purposes. It is useful to practice classifying a set of individual things in a number of ways, keeping the same general purpose for classification. This stimulates flexibility of outlook that is useful in making new classifications.

It may be helpful to ask ourselves the following questions about any classification we may make:

1. Have I left anything out?
2. Do any of my classes overlap?
3. Is it really clear why each thing is in the class I have put it in, or might some individuals just as well be in another class?
4. Is this classification really useful for my purpose? Might another classification be even more useful?

PITFALLS

Classification is something we all do every day. But like many things we do every day, we often do it badly. In this section we will look at some of the most common mistakes.

One very frequent fault, often committed by beginners in classification, is what I call the overstuffed miscellaneous. Suppose that a child, for example, begins to classify animals. He lists cats, dogs, horses, and cows, then running out of inspiration or energy makes his final class "other animals." Now in one sense this is a *complete* classification, since every animal is either a dog, a cat, a horse, a cow, or some other animal. But obviously that last class contains many more animals than all of the other classes put together, unless you had a group of animals consisting mostly of dogs, cats, horses, and cows, with a few squirrels and rabbits thrown in. In that case it might make sense to classify them this way, but in general, any classification that leaves a large number of individuals lumped together in an "other" or miscellaneous class is likely to be unsatisfactory.

We should, nonetheless, have a catchall miscellaneous class. If I am on an expense account while traveling on business, I may classify my major expenditures as transportation, hotel, meals, and, perhaps, phone calls. Then if I have a few minor expenditures that are hardly worth listing separately, I may lump them together as miscellaneous expenditures. But if I turn in an expense account in which miscellaneous expenditures amount to more than the major items, it is not likely to be approved.

Another common fault in classification is *forced classification*. Given some set of categories that may not be exhaustive or adequate for a certain purpose, we try to make the facts fit the classification rather than the classification fit the facts. This is a common fault of officials and administrators. An old English joke tells about a man in charge of the baggage car on a country train. His table of rates for transporting animals covered only a few common domestic animals, so he decreed that "a cat is a dog, and a rabbit is a dog, but a tortoise is an insect!" Of course, as a practical solution to the problem of how much to charge for animals not on the rate schedule, this is not at all absurd; it amounts to "Pay the same for a cat or rabbit as for a dog, but for transporting a tortoise pay the same rate as for a colony of bees." But it would seem that the railroad needed a more complete set of tariffs.

A forced classification that often hits close to home is the tendency of some teachers to classify their students in a few rigid categories (bright, troublemaker, underachiever, etc.) without considering the real complexities of human beings.

Another common fault is *overclassification*. This may occur because of overenthusiasm or fussiness, but it can also arise from carelessly putting each apparently new case into a new class without asking whether it might just as well have gone into a class already made. Such sprawling classifications are of little use. Any overelaborate classification may get in the way of its purpose.

Consider our earlier examples of clearing the land for the summer cabin and sorting the clothing for flood victims. A botanical classification of the vegetation site would be much too elaborate for the purpose we imagined. An overelaborate classification of the clothing might delay its distribution until it was too late to do any good. A flood victim might prefer to have a dry though too-large pair of pants when he was first rescued rather than get an exactly fitting pair the next day.

The opposite fault, *underclassification*, may be even more common. Putting individuals into a few simple classes is seldom helpful in dealing with a problem. The generalizations that begin "There are two kinds of people . . ." are almost always oversimplifications (except perhaps the one that says "There are two kinds of people. Those who divide people into two kinds of people, and those who don't").

Some common forms of underclassification are worth listing:

1. Thinking in ones: trying to explain everything in a situation in terms of one idea. All the people who explain whatever happens in terms of a conspiracy (Communist, Jewish, Fascist, revolutionary) are open to this charge. Of course some one philosophical or religious idea might explain everything, but a great deal of proof would be needed.

2. Dualism, or thinking in twos: trying to explain everything in some area in terms of some set of opposites. If the opposites are of the sort that logicians call *contraries*, then although they are mutually exclusive they will not be exhaustive—we can easily find a possibility not covered by either of the opposed pair. Black and white are opposite in this sense: nothing can be both black all over and at the same time and in the same way white all over. But plenty of things are neither black nor white. Another kind of opposite is the sort that logicians call *contradictories*. Black and not-black are contradictories since anything is either one or the other. But opposites that are contradictories always have one class which is enormously oversized; the class of not-black things, for example, includes everything in the universe but black things.

3. Thinking in threes, fours, etc. Simple classifications are dangerous because the facts may fail to conform to your set pattern. Situations, problems, and tasks have structures that we must understand if we are to deal with them adequately. As we said in our discussion of forced classification, when we impose some previously decided classification on the facts

instead of letting the facts decide the classification, we lose touch with reality.

Incidentally, you may have noticed, when you first looked at the table of contents to this book, that I am fond of dividing my chapters into three. I like to think this is just a teaching device and I am not led astray by it, but perhaps you should be on the lookout for any cases where my fondness for patterns may have misled me. Logicians tend to have tidy minds, but the universe is not always correspondingly tidy!

CASES

1. Assuming your purpose is to buy a home for a family, classify houses available in your area, trying to meet all four requirements for classification.

2. Assuming your purpose is to promote road safety, classify the important factors in road accidents. Be especially careful to avoid overlapping classes.

3. Without looking at the "Want Ads" section of your local paper, write out a classification you think might be adequate for such ads. Then look at the actual classification used by your paper. How many kinds of ads did you omit? Does the paper leave out any class of ads you included? Could you improve on the classification it uses? (Compare a large city paper and a small local paper: Do they use the same classification for ads? Does the smaller paper omit some classifications?)

4. Consider some publication connected with your work or interests, for example your college catalogue if you are a student, a record catalogue, a magazine you read regularly. How could the material be reorganized? Would the reorganization be an improvement? Are some classifications more or less forced on you by the nature of the subject matter?

5. Take some group of people known to you (for example friends, family, school class, etc.) and classify the group in two different ways, keeping the same general purpose for classification. State the purpose clearly. Which classification is more adequate to the purpose? Why?

CHAPTER 3
ORGANIZATION

FINDING THE ELEMENTS

The relation between classification and organization is that of part to whole; classification is one way but not the only way of organizing material. When we tell a story in chronological order or rank mountains by height we are organizing our material but not classifying it in the ordinary sense. We *could* possibly think of all organization as classification: In ranking mountains by height we could think of ourselves as putting mountains into classes according to height; in telling a story we could think of ourselves as putting events into classes according to time. But we would be stretching the idea of classification too much.

The reasons for organization are like the reasons for classification: to enable us to deal with material that would otherwise be messy and unmanageable. The dangers, too, are similar; we are tempted to oversimplify, to make the facts fit our pattern rather than the pattern fit the facts.

In organizing material, one problem we face at the beginning is that of finding which elements to organize. Suppose we want to give an organized account of the complex events surrounding the death of President Kennedy. The elements we are to organize are events, of course, but what events? Should we relate every relevant event that happened at a given time, even though these events are widely separated in space? Jim Bishop uses this method in *The Day Kennedy Died*. Or should we follow the more usual technique of presenting the actions of one major figure or one series of events with comments on minor happenings to fill in background? Depending on the method we use, some events may be fully described, partially described, or left out altogether. We must get clear about which events are important to us and choose a method of organization which enables us to do justice to these events.

In any attempt at organizing material we must begin by going through it, probably discarding some material and deciding on the relative importance of the rest. A familiar example is the cleaning of a house or room. Some things that have been lying around are thrown away, others are put in storage or where they can be got at easily, others are put in more prominent places.

An example of a different kind is the writing of a newspaper story. The reporter may note a great number of facts as he collects his information. When he writes up his notes he will usually find that some of this information is of no use for his story. The rest of the material must be organized in order of importance. Reporters often write stories in such a way that the essential facts are in the lead paragraph, and the information in the succeeding paragraphs is progressively less important. Thus if the story must be shortened, or if a hasty reader does not read the story to the end, the gist of the story will still get through.

The author of a textbook like this one has a similar problem. A great number of different things have been studied by logicians, but not all of them are useful for a book of this sort. Of the material that is appropriate, some is more important than the rest. Although the importance of a subject should be reflected in the amount of coverage given it, sometimes less important topics need extensive explanation. Thus the problem of just what to cover, just what elements to organize into a book, can be complex.

Often in organizing the material that is available to start with, we find that new material is needed. For example, the housecleaner throws away a rickety chair and finds that a replacement is needed. The reporter begins to organize his material and finds that a vital fact is missing. In this book the section you are reading now contains material not often found in logic books. The need to add such a section became apparent as I began to organize the book.

There are no set rules for finding elements to organize, but the following rules of thumb may be useful:

1. There must be a reasonably large accumulation of material to begin with. If there are only a few items, organizing them will not usually be necessary.
2. Some of the items will almost certainly have to be discarded. To tell the whole truth about even the simplest things is an ideal that is impossible in practice.
3. The items to be organized must themselves be relatively simple.
4. The items to be organized should not themselves be in need of internal organization. Imagine, for example, the difficulty of finding a name in the phone book if all names with the same first letter were listed together, but within each such group the names were listed helter-skelter.

ORDERING THE ELEMENTS

Once we have selected the elements to be organized we are usually faced with a number of possible ways of ordering or organizing the elements. Suppose you have got a new bookcase and want to put some order into your somewhat chaotic collection of books. You could simply arrange them according to size or color, but that is not likely to be very useful when you are looking for a book. To arrange them by subject would be useful for some purposes. Or you might arrange them alphabetically by author or title. (The alphabet is one of the great organizing devices invented by the human mind.) No arrangement is perfect; each is useful for some purposes.

In arranging events for a fictional or historical account we also have a number of choices. We can follow the advice of the King of Hearts to Alice and "Begin at the beginning, and when you get to the end, stop." Or we can begin with an exciting or vital event and go on from there, using flashbacks to fill in the background. (This is not a new technique; Homer used it with great skill in the *Iliad* and the *Odyssey*.) Or we can jump back and forth between past and future, although this technique can be confusing in the hands of an inexperienced writer. The beginning-to-end arrangement of events is usually called *chronological* order, but the more complex techniques are also chronological ways of ordering events. Therefore we will call the beginning-to-end technique *strict* chronological order. Strict chronological order is neither necessarily the best nor the worst technique for organizing an account of events. It is suitable for some accounts, unsuitable for others.

Events or facts can also be arranged in a number of other ways; for example, in order of increasing or decreasing importance. Objects can be arranged in a number of ways; for example, by size. If we look at an organized collection of facts such as an almanac we find all kinds of arrangements. We may find cities listed by population and rivers by length, which are measures of size. We may find a catalogue of important news stories of the year, listed in order of importance. We may also find a chronology for the year that lists important events in strict chronological order.

All of these and many more are legitimate ways of organizing material. What distinguishes organization from disorganization is that there is always *some* reason for the position of the item in the list or account. On the other hand, in a disorganized list or account, item *B* follows item *A* only because the compiler of the account or list happened to think of it at that time. A frequent fault of beginning writers and all but the best extemporaneous speakers is the "I forgot to say . . ." that introduces new material that should have been given earlier for better understanding. Thus the first piece of advice we can give for successfully organizing material is:

**1. Decide on the principle of organization
that you are going to use and
state it clearly (at least to yourself).**

Sometimes it is necessary to use more than one principle of organization, but if so, the relation between them should be made clear. Suppose that you list major cities of the United States by geographical area and size. You will get quite a different list depending on whether size or area is the first category. One list might start as follows:

Eastern Cities
Over 100,000
50,000–100,000
Etc.

The other list might read as follows:

Cities with over 100,000 Population
Eastern
Midwestern
Etc.

Again, other principles of organization may creep in unnoticed. Are we to list geographical areas by geographical position, East, Midwest, West, Pacific Coast, or are we to list them by population sizes? In the latter case, Pacific Coast would come before West. Thus the second piece of advice for organizing material is:

**2. Make it clear how many
principles of organization are being used,
and what relation they have to one another.**

The kind of organization you need depends on the purpose you have in organizing the material. Frequently in organizing information or objects, an important purpose is ease of retrieval—how quickly you can find the

item when you need it. But organization, like classification, can have many purposes. Sometimes we organize
in order to bring certain things into prominence. Some
people seem to feel that there is prestige in being high
on a list, even a list of most-wanted criminals or worst-
dressed women. We may organize material to brag "Our
city has the cleanest air of any major city" or to complain "Our state spends less for education than any
other state in this region." At any rate, it seems wise
to add this advice to our list:

3. **Choose a method of organization that serves
your purpose as well as possible and does not
hinder or defeat your purpose in organizing.**

We are all familiar with people and institutions that
are so overorganized or underorganized that they defeat their own purposes. Sam and Sally each set out
to paint a doghouse before dinner. Sam does not finish
because he has to keep going back to the cellar for a
forgotten paint brush, for something to open the paint
can, etc. Sally spends so much time getting her equip-
ment laid out, planning which side to paint first, etc.,
that she does not have enough time left to finish the
job either. The Do-good Foundation has the best of
intentions and lots of money, but is so disorganized
and inefficient that little help gets to those in need.
The Perfect Pencil Company is so overorganized that
its employees spend more time filling out forms and
going through unnecessary procedures than they do in
production work. All of these individuals and institutions could use our next piece of advice:

4. **Do not underorganize or overorganize.**

Use the simplest organization that is consistent with
your purposes, but remember that disorganized effort
is usually wasteful. Most of us have a tendency to
either overdo or underdo organization. Overorganized
types have given order and planning a bad name, while
underorganized people have made casualness and in-
formality suspect. Once we realize in what direction
our own failings lie we may be able to do something
about compensating for them.

PRESENTING THE ORDERED ELEMENTS

Living in a complex and technically advanced society, we are familiar with a great many tools for first organizing material and then presenting it. A filing cabinet, for example, aids us to organize material when it comes in, and to have it available in an organized form. This book has two organizing devices—an index and a table of contents—which are common nowadays, but were unknown a few centuries ago. Closets, drawers, etc., help to organize our possessions.

But very often getting material to other people in an organized form presents a special problem. We will talk mainly about presenting information in a spoken or written form, but there are similar problems and similar solutions in other areas such as the organized delivery of materials and objects.

A piece of frequently given advice is to organize the material to be presented in outline form, with major headings, subheadings, subsubheadings, and so on. For example, we might want to write an essay on the effects of the murder of President Kennedy. One division that might suggest itself could be between effects on individuals and effects on groups. After a certain amount of scribbling and thought, trying not to leave any individual or group out, we might find ourselves with an outline like this:

Effects of President Kennedy's Assassination

I. On individuals
  A. Individuals close to Kennedy
    1. Family
      a. Mrs. Kennedy
      b. Kennedy's children
      c. Kennedy's brothers and sisters
      d. Kennedy's parents
    2. Nonfamily
      a. Vice-President Johnson
      b. Kennedy's staff
      c. Kennedy cabinet members
  B. Individuals not close to Kennedy
    1. Involved in events of assassination

        a. Lee Harvey Oswald
        b. Jack Ruby
        c. Officer Tippit
        d. Governor Connally and Mrs. Connally
     2. Not involved in events of assassination
        a. Mrs. Oswald
        b. Ruby's family
        c. Tippit's family
        d. Governor Connally's family
II. On Groups
  A. Within the United States
     1. Friendly to Kennedy
        a. Democratic party
        b. Black leaders and civil rights forces
        c. Kennedy appointees and supporters in
           government
     2. Opposed in some way to Kennedy
        a. Republican party
        b. Segregationist forces
        c. Kennedy opponents in government
  B. Outside the United States
     1. Friendly to the United States
        a. Supporters of South Vietnamese government
        b. South Americans involved in Alliance for
           Progress
        c. Western Europeans
     2. Not friendly to the United States
        a. Viet Cong and North Vietnamese
        b. Cubans
        c. Russians

While far from complete, this outline could serve as the basis for a fairly detailed discussion of the effects of the Kennedy assassination. Of course the same material could be organized in other ways, but there is something to be said for making this distinction between effects on individuals and effects on groups. The headings of these major divisions are given Roman numerals, as is usual in outlines. The individuals could fall into various categories, but close to and not close to Kennedy seems an obviously important division, and these subheadings are marked by capital letters. The

same principle of organization could not be carried
over to the material under II, so under the capital-
lettered divisions there are groups inside and outside
the United States. The point illustrated here is that
we often have to use different principles of subdivision
within different parts of the outline.

In subdividing further, it seems that among individuals close to Kennedy, family and nonfamily are
the obvious principle of division; these are given Arabic
numbers. But for individuals not close to Kennedy the
corresponding numbers belong to those involved or
not involved in the assassination events. Notice that
here the division is somewhat arbitrary. Is Ruby to be
considered involved in the assassination events because
he killed Oswald, and Tippit because he was killed by
Oswald? Are Mrs. Oswald and Mrs. Tippit to be considered not involved? Since Ruby and Tippit did things
that affected events, there seems some basis for this
division, but whether Mrs. Oswald was actively involved depends on the facts of the case. Thus even in
organizing facts we are forced to make some judg-
ments about what the facts *are*.

In the division of groups, perhaps the greatest problem is to determine just what groups to include. Demo-
crats and Republicans were obviously affected, and so
were Kennedy supporters and opponents in government. But the effect on civil rights and anti–civil rights
forces is partly a matter of historical judgment. Again,
in the groups listed outside the United States, an
effort was made to include those importantly affected.
No doubt there were effects in Africa, Australia, and
the Middle East, but it can be argued that the effects
on the groups listed were more important and far-
reaching.

Now an outline like this might be a valuable aid
in organizing our thinking about the effects of Kennedy's death. But that does not mean it is the best way
to present the results of our thinking. For example, an
article using this outline as a basis might start out
by using some of the more dramatic results of the
assassination to catch the reader's attention. Imagine

an article written in 1978, reviewing the effects of Kennedy's death:

The Kennedy Assassination—15 Years Later

The bullet that ended the life of John Fitzgerald Kennedy on November 22, 1963, affected many other lives, directly or indirectly. Within hours, Officer Tippit would die seeking his assassin. Within days, Lee Harvey Oswald, the man who allegedly fired the bullet, would die. Lyndon Johnson would step from obscurity and powerlessness back to prominence and power. He would carry a civil rights bill through Congress partly on the emotional impact of Kennedy's death, and this would affect the climate of the years to come. Johnson would also make decisions about Vietnam that would affect thousands of Asians who had never heard of Kennedy. There would be reverberations in Castro's Cuba and in the chancelleries of Western Europe.

Looking back after 15 years . . .

The author of such an article might eventually cover all the points listed in our outline, but if he merely filled out the outline the article might be dull although clear. On the other hand, if he did not think out what he wanted to say in an organized way he would undoubtedly write a confused, disorganized piece, forgetting important points, and so on.

However, not everyone works best with an outline such as the one in our example. Some highly creative people find that an outline inhibits their spontaneity. J. B. Priestley, the English dramatist and novelist, describes one of his plays, *The Bad Samaritan*, in this way:

It was a sardonic comedy with a good basic idea, but it had a messy third act, and indeed needed not only rewriting but entirely reshaping. Ironically enough, this was the only one of my plays which I have ever written in the manner of the text-books, first building up a detailed synopsis, then clothing each scene with dialogue. The result was that my real imagination never got to work anywhere; it was all done with the surface of my mind, like a film script; so craftily and coldly put together that nowhere was there any life in it.[1]

Priestley's synopsis, of course, was not like our outline, but many people find that any kind of outline or synopsis has a similar deadening effect on their imagination. For such people, a first draft, sloppily organized, containing afterthoughts and so on, can be the best way to get their thoughts down on paper. This first draft can then be ruthlessly revised and rewritten. Some people can write clear, readable prose at the first attempt, even without outlines or synopses. But most of us are not so fortunate and need all the help we can get from outlines or revised drafts to write in a clear, organized way.

CASES

1. Suggest at least one other way of outlining the effects of the Kennedy assassination. Give a detailed outline comparable to the one in the text.

2. Consider some organized procedure that is familiar to you, for example, registration for classes if you attend college, the procedures of some job you have held, etc. First describe the procedure. What are the elements to be organized? What are the principles of organization? Then work out a different way of organizing these elements. Is your way an improvement? Why or why not?

3. Find some set of elements that so far as you know has not been organized (for example subjects of popular songs, types of chairs, uses for dowel rods). Organize these elements in some way. Could your organization of these elements be useful in any way? How? To whom?

[1]*Rain on Godshill*, Harper & Row, New York, 1939, p. 29.

4. Take some piece of writing that seems to you to be clear and well organized. Try to reconstruct an outline the author might have used to write the piece. Does your attempt at outlining reveal any inconsistencies or omissions in the piece?

5. Take some piece of writing that seems to you to be unclear and badly organized. What are the elements the author is trying to organize? What is the reason for his difficulties? Try to reorganize the same elements, doing a better job than the author of the piece.

PART TWO
CRITICISM

In this section we look at three kinds of difficulties that are encountered in argument. Since our assumptions often stand in the way of a solution to a problem, we must be aware of the presuppositions and prejudices which we may bring to a problem, and carefully consider the point of our activities. Since we may be misled by fallacious arguments, we should be aware of the common fallacies and know how to identify them. Since we may sometimes be tempted to put too much weight on weak arguments, we should become familiar with some of the kinds of argument that tend to be pushed too far, and know their weaknesses. Arguments from authority, from analogy and certain kinds of explanations by untested hypotheses are examples of these weak arguments. The aim of this section is to make your thinking more careful and critical, and to help you to avoid being misled by assumptions or by weak or fallacious arguments.

CHAPTER 4
ASSUMPTIONS

PRESUPPOSITIONS

It is almost impossible to approach any subject with a completely open mind. Even if it were possible it usually would not be desirable. How could I even get through breakfast unless I assumed that milk will not poison me, that a hot toaster will burn my hand, that butter will spread and not explode, and so on? But in order to think critically we must be aware of just what assumptions we are making and what grounds we have for making them. When we look for the grounds of our assumptions we sometimes find that there are no grounds except habit or custom. For example, we see a quietly dressed stranger walk confidently over to a parked car, get in, and after a few minutes drive away. We assume that he is the owner of the car. But what real grounds do we have for this assumption? It might be that the man is a car thief, and that if we looked closely at what he was doing after he got into the car we would find that he was crossing the wires.

This is an example of an assumption created or encouraged by a situation. We should also be aware of the assumptions common to our culture—our society, country, or class. The idea that anything old or traditional is therefore good is one which we find in some societies, and we correctly see that this assumption is unfounded. Some old or traditional things like fire-places or sleigh rides are good and enjoyable; some old and traditional things like torture or slavery are evil and horrible.

It is easy enough to see that the assumptions of another culture are open to question. But when it comes to our own society, we are often not aware that there *are* assumptions, much less that they are open to question. For example, a common assumption in our society is that anything new or original is likely to be better than what is old or traditional. But this is no more true than the opposite assumption. Some new things such as improved medical techniques are good and desirable. Other new things such as wide-spread pollution are bad and undesirable. But notice how often in our society *new* is used as a term of praise: "Buy *new* Splash detergent! Completely new formula!" Sometimes the ads say "new, improved Splash," but often the assumption is made that if a thing is new it is improved.

You might think that this is a reasonable assump-tion. But not all changes are improvements. New formula Splash may have a cheaper, less effective in-gredient substituted for one of the former ingredients, and be packaged in a smaller quantity for the same old price. Consumer research societies have found pre-cisely this situation more than once.

Another source of questionable assumptions is half-understood or misunderstood science. A good example of this is the "gambler's fallacy." Suppose that some-one is tossing a fair coin. Heads have come up fifty-seven times, tails forty-one times. Which is most likely to come up next time—heads or tails? The answer is that tails is no more likely to come up than heads on the next throw. (This is what is meant by calling the coin a *fair* coin.) If you said that tails is more likely to come up you were the victim of a widespread misconception, the gambler's fallacy, or the doctrine of the maturity of chances, as it is sometimes called. The source of this fallacy is a misunderstanding of what probability theory tells us about the long-run frequency of heads and tails in throws of a fair coin.

Nothing we have said should be taken as meaning that our assumptions are always mistaken or that we cannot often find a good reason for assumptions which we have made, even if we make them without much thought. Nor do we mean that you should check every assumption you find yourself making, no matter how trivial. It may not be your business whether the man getting into the car is its owner or not. If you challenge him he may quite rightly question your authority to do so. If you never buy detergents it may not matter to you whether Splash is improved or not. If you never gamble, the gambler's fallacy may be of no interest.

However, when making up our minds about anything of importance we should try to be aware of what assumptions we are making and what backing these assumptions have. There are a variety of ways to do this. For example, the best way to avoid false assumptions based on misunderstood science is to have a basic knowledge of important areas of science. This is one purpose of required general courses in colleges. But the person who does not have the opportunity of taking college courses can find many good books that will help him get a basic understanding of science. Many of these are entertaining as well as useful. For example, Darrell Huff's books *How to Lie with Statistics* and *How to Take a Chance*[1] are fun to read and will clear up many common confusions in the areas of probability and statistics. Irving Adler is another author noted for his clear and interesting explanations of science.[2]

Anthropologists tell us that actually living in a society very different from our own is the best way to recognize and question the assumptions of our own culture. Few of us have a chance to do this, but reading about people different from ourselves and ideas

[1] Norton, New York, 1954, 1960.
[2] For example, *The New Mathematics* and *Tools of Science*, John Day, New York, 1958.

different from our own can be at least a partial substitute.

The assumptions created or encouraged by a situation can sometimes be spotted by a similar tactic. If we try to look at a situation with completely new eyes, as a stranger or even as a man from Mars, we can often see that we are making assumptions about the situation that are not justified. One reason that many people enjoy science fiction is that it gives them a fresh slant on familiar institutions, problems, and situations.

It is also good practice to take some statement or situation and see how many assumptions we can find in it. For example, take a statement like "I want my daughter to go into television, so she'll make lots of money and be happy." This statement assumes that people in television make lots of money, which is not always true. It also seems to assume that making a lot of money will make someone happy, which does not seem to be borne out by the facts. But it also assumes that the speaker has, or at least plans to have, a daughter, a point so simple that it is easy to overlook.

When we ask whether a given thing is being assumed by a situation or statement, a good rule of thumb is to ask ourselves whether the statement or situation would make sense if the supposed assumption were false.

Consider a man who has trouble with his television set and determines to do something about it. He gets some tools and a ladder and starts climbing up to the roof. Unless we assume that his television set has a roof antenna, that he believes the trouble is with the antenna, and that he has at least some hope of fixing the antenna, his action would seem to make no sense. He also seems to be assuming that the ladder is safe, the roof will bear him, and so on.

Of course fuller knowledge of a situation or of the context of a statement may cause us to change our ideas about what assumptions are being made. What is assumed by a given statement or situation is seldom an absolute matter, but it does not need to be, for our purposes. All we need to be sure of is that we are not presupposing anything that is not justified by the evidence available to us.

PREJUDICES

We will define a prejudice as an assumption or presupposition that we are extremely reluctant to change or reject, even in the face of considerable evidence. We can be prejudiced in favor of persons or ideas as well as against them. Thus our meaning of prejudice will not be as weak as one dictionary definition of prejudice, "a judgment or opinion formed before the facts are known." But our definition is weaker than another dictionary definition, "a judgment or opinion held in disregard of facts that contradict it." Sometimes *bias* is used instead of *prejudice* for the meaning we have in mind, but *bias* can also have both meanings the dictionary gives to *prejudice*.

Prejudices are by definition illogical. It is not prejudice to assume that someone who has proved himself trustworthy on many occasions is trustworthy even when appearances are against him. It is not prejudice to suspect that someone with a long record of crimes may be guilty of another crime, even if we have no evidence to begin with. But a feeling for or against a person or idea for which we can give *no* rational backing is at least a bias, and if we are reluctant to change it in the face of evidence it is a prejudice, as we are using the term.

Perhaps, then, a completely reasonable person would have no prejudices. But most of us are equipped with a large set of prejudices for and against various people and ideas. Their origin may often be a matter for the psychologist. The reasons for getting rid of them are a matter for the moralist, and have to do with ethical considerations such as justice and impartiality. But the logician may be of some practical use in helping us to get rid of them. (Of course if our prejudices are neurotic or psychotic we need a psychiatrist, not a logician).

Since prejudice often thrives on ignorance, one useful rule for overcoming a prejudice is to become more familiar with the object of it. Advocates of integrating

the public schools use as one of their arguments the
contention that if children become familiar with each
other in the public school setting, they will learn to
see the falsity of racial stereotypes and begin to overcome racial prejudices.

Unfortunately, however, proximity does not always
mean familiarity. One way in which prejudice feeds
itself is by twisting facts to suit a preconceived pattern. While real familiarity with persons or ideas may
remove prejudices against them, mere exposure to
these persons or ideas may feed prejudice. Since everyone and everything has at least some negative aspects
(or at least seems to have such aspects), a person can
seize on these to support his prejudiced attitude.

Thus a more useful rule for overcoming prejudices
is to take the object of prejudice out of its familiar
context in some way, so that it can be seen anew. This
is one reason why racial prejudices sometimes seem
to be overcome more easily in college. Meeting members of other ethnic groups against a new background,
removed from familiar social backgrounds, sometimes
makes it possible to see them simply as persons to be
judged on their own merits.

Where ideas are in question, it is sometimes possible to place them in new contexts by studying their
historical development or comparing them with similar
ideas.

Finally, we can sometimes overcome prejudices by
a deliberate effort to create a counterprejudice. This
often works where some group has accepted an unfavorable view of itself held by some other group; in
effect it has a prejudice against itself. What is then
sometimes possible is to create a counterprejudice by
emphasizing every favorable aspect of the group. In
the struggle which led to the establishment of the
Irish Republic, a considerable emphasis was put on
the glories of Irish history, Irish art, and so on. This
helped to create national pride and overcome feelings
of defeatism and hopelessness. Similar efforts are now
going on in the Black, Chicano, Chinese, and other com-
munities in America. It is pointless to criticize these

attempts to create a counterprejudice as one-sided. But
there are obvious dangers outside the group. Counterprejudice may reinforce the prejudice against which it
is directed rather than neutralize it. The dangers inside
the group are those of any attitude not based on fact
—to be prejudiced is not to see things as they are, and
reality may take its revenge.

Ideally, familiarity, seeing the object in new contexts, and the neutralization of prejudice by counterprejudice should leave us without prejudices. But our
favorable or unfavorable attitudes may not be altered.
Closer familiarity with the philosophy of some group
or with the group itself may give us good reasons to
distrust or dislike it. To detest the Mafia for good and
sufficient reasons is not prejudice. It may in fact be
our duty.

PRECONDITIONS

An assumption, as we have said, could be detected by
the fact that without it a statement or situation would
make no sense. Philosophers have tried to find certain
absolute preconditions or presuppositions of all experience or of all meaningful language. They have argued
that without certain logical principles we could not
speak meaningfully or act meaningfully. Without going
this deep, we can usefully consider the assumptions
which must be made for certain areas of activity to be
meaningful.

For example, a great deal of activity in our society
is based on the assumption that progress, by which is
meant increased production and consumption of material goods, is always desirable. Pollution and the danger of exhausting our natural resources have caused
many people to begin to challenge this assumption. But
it is still behind a great deal of what goes on in our
society.

A similarly widespread and basic assumption in our
society is that it is justifiable to spend large amounts
of time and money and risk injury and even death for
the sake of certain kinds of enjoyment. The amounts
of time and money spent on sports in countries like

the United States or Australia would be completely in-
comprehensible to many societies of the past and even
to some present-day societies.

Basic assumptions are especially important because
many of the most serious arguments, among the most
difficult to resolve, arise from differences in fundamental assumptions. Such differences exist between
Communist and non-Communist societies, between Eastern and Western societies. At present we can readily
observe the effect of different assumptions in arguments between people belonging to different genera-
tions. It is important to realize this condition since
arguments about subsidiary points that do not get at
the preconditions of the dispute have almost no chance
of being settled reasonably.

For example, consider a typical argument between
parents and a teen-ager about hair length or clothing
styles. There is very little chance of settling such a
dispute in a reasonable way unless both sides realize
that there are fundamental differences in basic assumptions. In a case like this it very often happens
that behind the parents' attitude are certain assumptions about the importance of conformity for success
in life, and certain assumptions about what success
in life consists of. These may be based on experience;
for example, parents of immigrant background may
have experienced the condition that immigrants who
conformed to the society around them were able to
achieve their objectives successfully, while those who
failed to conform were not. This assumption may or
may not be outdated, but the parents are likely to
hold to it emotionally without being fully aware of
why they feel so strongly. The teen-ager's rejection of
this assumption may be based on the fact that he cannot see any foundation for it, or may be based merely
on impatience or inability to foresee the consequence
of certain decisions.

Similarly, the parents' assumption that material success (financial security and a comfortable life) is a
worthy purpose for life may be based on their own
feelings of satisfaction at having gained this kind of

success, perhaps in the face of great difficulties. They may fail to recognize that a goal is satisfying when one struggles to attain it for himself, but may seem less important if it is readily attainable. The teen-ager's rejection of material success as a goal may arise from a reasoned preference for some other life-style, or may be merely a rejection of a situation that he identifies with subordination and powerlessness for himself. In both cases, associations and emotions may play a great part. As in the case of verbal disputes, merely finding the real basis of disagreement will not magically resolve the argument. But it will offer a better chance for resolving it.

A word we often use in discussing the assumptions which underlie activity is *point*. When we ask "What is the point of that?" we are often presenting the challenge "*Is* there any point to that?" The point of an activity is often its purpose or end result. "What was the point of shooting that gun in the air?" "I was trying to attract his attention, and that was the only way to do it." "What was the point of cutting down that tree?" "Now I get sunlight in the windows on that side of the house." Where the point of an activity is a purpose or end result, the assumption we are making is that the purpose is a worthwhile one or the end result is worth achieving.

When we find ourselves in conflict over basic assumptions, it is sometimes possible to find an even more basic assumption that will enable us to resolve the dispute. The United States and Russia differ completely about what sort of society is desirable, but can cooperate in certain areas because they both agree that all-out nuclear warfare must be avoided. Parents and children can sometimes find common values that will enable them to settle their disputes.

Ultimately, questions about basic assumptions lead back to the sort of questions considered by philosophers. Whether life has a point or is pointless, whether pleasure is the only goal worth seeking, whether material success is a worthy goal for life—these are all questions that have been considered from the beginning of philosophy. But to consider such questions would take us far beyond the relatively modest and practical aims of this book.

CASES

1. Find all the assumptions you can in the following statement: "I would never want my children to ruin their lives by using drugs."

2. What assumptions can you find in the following situation: A man who has no meat in the house takes a rifle out of his closet, leans out his window, and shoots at a squirrel.

3. Take a statement from the front page of a current newspaper, preferably a statement made by some prominent national figure. Find all the assumptions you can in this statement. Are all of these assumptions justified?

4. Consider some activity that you yourself have often engaged in. What is the point of this activity? How would you justify this activity to someone who challenged your engaging in it?

5. What other suggestions can you make for overcoming prejudice? Identify the sort of prejudice you are concerned with and try to make your suggestions concrete and practical. Be specific.

CHAPTER 5
FALLACIES

A fallacy, it is generally agreed, is an argument that in fact is not a good argument, but for some reason appears convincing. The first person to study logic systematically, the Greek philosopher Aristotle, began the practice of listing common fallacies, and many logic books imitate Aristotle by including such a list. Unfortunately most such lists have grown unmanageably long and are not organized very systematically. Some lists include mistakes that are not mistakes in *argument*, and many of the fallacies in the traditional lists overlap each other.

In this chapter, we will try to give you some idea of the common arguments that have not already been discussed and that will not be discussed in later chapters. Like most such discussions, it is somewhat of a grab bag of fallacies which do not fit neatly under any other division of logic. Fallacies that result from ambiguity or vagueness have already been discussed in Chapter 1; fallacies of induction and deduction will be discussed in Part Three, and so on. Thus the fallacies discussed in this chapter are the leftovers. I have tried to organize them as well as possible rather than give the usual helter-skelter list, and I try to say something about *why* they are deceptively convincing.

The terminology which logicians have invented in
their attempts to classify fallacies is somewhat complicated. Aristotle's Greek terms were translated (and
sometimes mistranslated) into Latin, and these in turn
have been translated more or less loosely into English.
Some of these terms have made their way into ordinary
language, and it may be useful for you to be familiar
with a few of them.

NOT THE POINT

The first sort of fallacy which we will discuss has the
technical name *non sequitur*, which is Latin for "it
does not follow." We sometimes encounter this term
in stories or essays, for example "His argument was a
mere *non sequitur*." (For some reason *non sequiturs*
are often "mere" in literary contexts.) We will call
fallacies of this type *Not the Point* fallacies, since in
this type of invalid argument the premises have no
real connection with the conclusion. We also will give
each subtype of fallacy a name (where possible the
traditional name), but it is more important to be
able to see what is wrong with a fallacious argument
than to be able to label it. In most real-life arguments,
labeling a fallacy is of little use, but being able to explain what is wrong with the argument may win your
point.

The first fallacy of this kind which we will consider
is the *Fallacy of Association* in which there is no real
connection between the premises and the conclusion
of the argument, and the argument *seems* convincing
because of associations established by habit, custom,
or some similar conditioning. Common examples of
this sort of fallacy can be found in advertisements. If
we regard advertisements as arguments whose conclusion is something like "our product is the best buy,"
then we find that many of them are very bad arguments. They try to establish an association between
their product and things that we regard favorably such
as springtime, pretty girls and handsome men, love and
romance, and so on. But when we look carefully at the
supposed connection, we often find that it does not
exist logically. A common type of advertisement con-

sists of a picture of a pretty girl sitting on the fender
of a new car, or holding a tube of toothpaste, or drinking a soft drink. Often the advertisements consist of
little more than this. But what is the connection between the girl and the product?

In sober fact, the girl is a professional model, well
paid to sit on the car or hold the advertiser's product.
Other pretty girls may or may not be impressed by
that car or use that toothpaste. But the attempt is
made to establish the association in our minds. Similarly, cigarette advertisements which show he-men
such as cowboys, steel workers, or hunters smoking
the cigarette are trying to establish a connection in our
minds between the product and masculinity. But even
if it were true that many he-men smoked that cigarette,
they might have a variety of reasons. It might be
cheaper, more easily available in some areas, or something of the sort. And even if he-men Abe, Bill, and
Charley all liked the cigarette, he-man Don might
hate it.

Perhaps we should not regard advertisements as
very good examples of argumentation. Still, in many
arguments in politics, religion, and everyday life we
find similar tactics being used. In our society a position
is often argued against on the basis that it is "Communist." In Communist societies, the bad word is bour-
geois, and so on. An especially silly example of this
kind of argument occurred when the Nazis dismissed
Einstein's work in physics as "Jewish thinking."

The prejudice appealed to may be against a group
or against an individual. In this form it is sometimes
called the ad hominem fallacy or Fallacy of Personal
Attack. Even where the prejudice has some foundation,
it is silly to dismiss an idea simply because you dislike
its source. Bad men can have good ideas. Right-wing
writers often point out that a graduated income tax is
a Communist idea. This is true to the extent that a demand for such a tax is included in a list of ten demands
in the Communist Manifesto. But also in that list is a
demand for laws against the exploitation of child labor!
If we oppose Communism must we favor child labor?
There may indeed be cases where it is legitimate to

attack individuals or groups. If a man is running for public office, for example, his faults and even his weaknesses may be fair game for exposure. If a group such as the Mafia or the Ku Klux Klan is performing illegal acts it is a right and even a duty to attack them. But if we reject *ideas* because of their source, we are really putting ourselves at the mercy of those we oppose. If our enemies praise a thing, we find ourselves pushed into damning it. Party politics offers many instances of such absurdities. Opposing a position just because your enemies hold it is called the *Fallacy of Opposition.*

More subtle forms of the same fallacy occur in cases where an idea is downgraded by making it seem funny (the *Fallacy of Ridicule*) or because it is new and untried, or because it is old and outworn, or because it is unpopular. Such fallacies can be lumped together as *ad populem* fallacies, or the *Fallacy of Appeal to Popular Prejudice.* In all of these cases, as soon as we really look at the proposed argument, we can see that the conclusion simply does not follow from the premises. Consider our reaction if we were simply presented an argument that such and such is false because

1. It is funny.
2. It is an old idea.
3. It is a new idea.
4. It is an unpopular idea.

Only because the argument is not presented explicitly *as* an argument, or only because the inadequacy of the argument is disguised by rhetoric or appeals to emotion, can such arguments deceive anyone. Once we bring the reasoning out into the open, we can see that the conclusion does not follow. We realize that ideas like the roundness of the earth or the possibility of space travel were once regarded as funny. We can see that old ideas, such as the necessity of food and sleep, can be true, and so can new ideas, such as the danger of pollution. Many ideas which are now commonplace truisms were once unpopular (though this does not mean that every unpopular idea will become a truism).

An appropriate, though not very polite, reply to most arguments of the kind we have been considering is simply "So what?" The girl in the ad is pretty, but so what? She makes the product no better or worse. The person putting forward the view may be unpleasant, but so what? The view may still be correct, and it is foolish to neglect the possibility. If there is a reply to the "So what?" be wise enough to listen to it. But in many cases there really is none.

BESIDE THE POINT

In another large class of bad arguments *some* conclusion is proved, but not the one which seems to be proved. (We do not always mean this error when we criticize an argument as being beside the point, but when it is, *Beside the Point Fallacy* will be a convenient label.) Such arguments are convincing because it is often easy to confuse what was actually proven with what was supposed to be proven. This fallacy is technically called *ignoratio elenchi*, an almost untranslatable phrase. Literally it means something like misunderstanding of what has been proved or disproved, and the account we have given of the Beside the Point fallacies agrees with most accounts of this fallacy. Except among logicians this cumbersome and puzzling phrase has never had much currency. Subdivisions of this fallacy have their own names, and are sometimes grouped together as Fallacies of Relevance.

A subdivision of this kind of fallacy is called the *Fallacy of Irrelevant Conclusion.* As an example, suppose someone argues that women are exploited and discriminated against. In reply, surveys and other evidence are presented to show that many women do not *feel* that they are exploited and discriminated against. This reply is beside the point in two ways. First, the fact that many women do not feel exploited or discriminated against leaves open the possibility that many others *do.* Second, even if all but a small minority did not feel exploited or discriminated against, their feeling is not proof that they are not really exploited or discriminated against. Most people tend to accept what they are used to, and the mere fact that a group does not complain does not prove that it has nothing to complain about.

Advertisers are frequent users of this sort of bad argument. That a stomach pill neutralizes an unspecified amount of acid in a test tube does not mean that it will efficiently neutralize acid in your stomach, or that it might not have undesirable side effects. That a razor blade can be shown to shave lather off a balloon without bursting it does not mean that it will not cut or scratch a face in the less expert hands of the average shaver. That tablet A dissolves faster than tablet B in a glass of water does not mean that the rate at which they dissolve in your stomach will be significantly different. But we are so easily impressed by what we see with our own eyes that we may forget to ask whether what we have seen proves what was supposed to be proved.

A common type of beside the point argument, called the *Fallacy of Unqualified Generalization*, consists of those arguments which establish a fact about only some members of a class while claiming to establish it about all of the members of that class, or at least about most members of that class. Often a whole race or group— Negroes, Jews, welfare recipients—is condemned on the basis of evidence that, if it proves anything, proves something about only a few members of the group. Members of the white majority are now finding with a shock that this kind of argument is being applied to them by members of minority groups. Because some whites have mistreated or exploited minorities, members of these minorities blame all whites. The argument is equally illogical in whichever direction the blame is pointed, though perhaps more understandable when used in self-defense by minorities.

Another common type of beside the point argument creates, at best, the *probability* that a conclusion is true, but is treated as if it created a certainty. A frequently encountered subclass of this type of argument, called the *post hoc ergo propter hoc* fallacy or *Fallacy of "After, Therefore Because,"* has to do with causes. One piece of evidence that we consider in deciding whether

A is the cause of *B* is that *A* has frequently or always been observed to precede *B*. Of course, not everything that precedes a given event is a cause of the event. Almost every baby cuts some teeth before learning to walk, but the appearance of the teeth is not the cause of the walking. When we argue that *A* preceded *B*, therefore *A* caused *B*, we are jumping from evidence which at best creates a probability that *A* is the cause of *B*, to a conclusion which is treated as a certainty.

Another kind of Beside the Point Fallacy is the *Fallacy of Arguing from Ignorance*. An argument that at best proves that a conclusion has not been disproved is used to attempt to establish that conclusion. For example, "All efforts to show that there is no monster in Loch Ness have failed. Therefore we must conclude that there *is* a monster in Loch Ness." Even if it is true that all efforts to disprove the existence of the Loch Ness monster have been unsuccessful, our conclusion should be that the question is still open, not that the existence of the monster is thereby proved. Many arguments of this kind can be neatly reversed: We might just as well argue that "All efforts to prove the existence of a monster in Loch Ness have failed. Therefore there is certainly no monster in Loch Ness." The one argument is no better than the other.

Both these arguments may seem convincing because we unconsciously add some further premise to them: "If the monster did not exist, its nonexistence would have been proved by now" in the one case, and "If the monster did exist its existence would have been proved by now" in the second. But such premises are often hard to establish, and unless we can establish one or the other of them, the mere failure to prove or disprove leads to no positive conclusion.

A final type of Beside the Point Fallacy, the *Fallacy of Circumstances*, occurs when an argument that proves at best that a conclusion is true normally in ordinary circumstances, or where there has been no change in circumstances, is used in an attempt to show that a conclusion is true in abnormal or extraordinary or changed circumstances. For example, "My client has driven for many years without an accident and has

never even received a traffic citation. Surely this proves
that he could not be at fault in this accident." The
reply to this might be: "Your client's past record is
beside the point. Our tests show that he was definitely
drunk at the time of the accident."

In all cases of Bedside the Point fallacies it may very
well be the case that *something* is proved. But that
something is not the point at issue, although they are
related in some way. If we are content to scale down
our claims and admit that we have established less
than we at first thought we had, a good deal can often
be salvaged from such arguments.

BEYOND THE POINT

The fallacy that we will call the *Beyond the Point
Fallacy* consists of assuming that the point at issue has
been proved, and going on to draw further conclusions
on the basis of this assumption. It is among those
classified by logicians under the general head of *petitio
principii*, somewhat puzzlingly rendered into English
as *begging the question*. The Latin phrase and Aristotle's Greek phrase, which it translates, mean something like assuming the starting point or assuming the
point in question; begging the question means just this.
The phrase is sometimes used outside logic, though it is
seldom used correctly. One variety of this fallacy is the
Fallacy of Arguing in a Circle. One modern logician
gives the following amusing example of arguing in a
circle:

> *What makes you think Lefty is a crook?*
> *Well, look at the crooks he associates with.*
> *How do you know they're crooks?*
> *Well, anyone who'd associate with a crook like
>   Lefty . . .*

Lefty is a crook because he associates with certain people; they are crooks because they associate with Lefty.
Wherever you start you go round and round. Arguing
in a circle sometimes occurs in real arguments, but less
often than the fallacy we have called the Beyond the
Point Fallacy.

Where this assumption is an unconscious one, both

parties may be confused or misled, and we have the sort of situation that we discussed in our chapter on assumptions. But often the person who is putting forward an argument of this type is well aware that the conclusion has not really been proved, and is trying to confuse or mislead others. We will call this the *Fallacy of the Assumed Premise*.

Advertisements which appeal to snobbery often use this tactic: "Of course our product is the very best, so a discriminating person like yourself will naturally want to use it." Politicians, too, are familiar with this tactic: By assuming that their points have already been proved they can sometimes convince the electorate to do so. They can then build on these points.

Either variety of this fallacy, if carried off with conviction and finesse, can be a very effective trick of argument. When a point is treated as already proved, it tends to create a sort of illusion in our minds that it *has* been proved.

Words or phrases such as *of course, obviously, it is clear,* often mark attempts to assume that some controversial point has in fact been proved or that it can be taken for granted. Sometimes an *of course* or an *obviously* is unobjectionable, as in "Of course not everyone reasons logically" or "Obviously some people are more intelligent than others." But it would not be a bad thing if our hackles rose slightly at every *of course* and we looked suspiciously at every phrase beginning *obviously* or *it is clear*.

We can summarize the fallacies we have examined as follows:

Types of Fallacy
  I. Not the Point fallacies *(non sequitur)*
    1. Fallacy of Association
    2. Fallacy of Personal Attack *(ad hominem)*
    3. Fallacy of Opposition
    4. Fallacy of Ridicule
    5. Fallacy of Appeal to Popular Prejudice *(ad populem)*
  II. Beside the Point fallacies *(ignoratio elenchi)*
    1. Fallacy of Irrelevant Conclusion

2. Fallacy of Unqualified Generalization
3. Fallacy of "After, Therefore Because" (*post hoc ergo propter hoc*)
4. Fallacy of Arguing from Ignorance
5. Fallacy of Circumstances
III. Beyond the Point fallacies (*petitio principii*)
   1. Fallacy of Arguing in a Circle
   2. Fallacy of the Assumed Premise

It is sometimes possible to avoid fallacies by *limiting the discussion*. This technique is most useful in formal debates and arguments but may be of some use even in ordinary conversation. To limit the discussion, we try to get clear answers to these questions before starting a discussion:

1. What are we trying to prove?
2. What would be acceptable as proof?
3. Can we here and now produce an acceptable proof?

By answering the first question clearly and fully we guard ourselves to some extent against arguments that are beside the point. By answering the second we make it harder to introduce completely irrelevant evidence, as in Not the Point fallacies. The combination of questions 1 and 2 makes it harder to assume the point in question and argue about matters that are beyond the point. The third question helps to avoid discussions that could be settled, but not by any evidence that is immediately available. Arguing about matters that could be settled by a dictionary, a record book, etc., when these are not available is a waste of everyone's time. Similarly, arguments about the distant future, the unrecorded past, and other inaccessible areas are not likely to reach any useful conclusion. If they are engaged in purely for amusement, no harm is done. But too often the hottest arguments are about points that there is no way to settle.

I do not include under this heading religious, political, or philosophical arguments. Reasonable answers to questions of this sort are available, if we have the patience and discipline to approach them properly. In fact, the study of logic is one valuable preliminary to a disciplined approach to such questions.

CASES

1. Go through a recent issue of a mass-circulation magazine, such as *Time*, *Life*, *Saturday Review*, etc. How many advertisements in the magazine commit the Not the Point Fallacy? How many are guilty of the Beside the Point Fallacy? How many assume the point at issue and go beyond the point? If you crossed out or tore out every ad or portion of an ad which committed these fallacies, how much would be left? How would you classify this remaining material?

2. Watch television for several hours and keep some kind of record of the commercials. Try to classify the fallacies committed in these commercials.

3. Gather a selection of political advertisements and arguments. (If it is not near election time look at back issues of newspapers at the time of the last election.) Can you find in these advertisements any of the fallacies we have discussed? Are details about a candidate's family relevant to his suitability for public office? What about other details of his biography such as military service, schooling, etc.?

4. Try to get hold of one of the newspapers or newsletters issued by an extremist group on the right or left. What sort of evidence is offered for the assertions made? Can you find in this material any of the fallacies which we have discussed?

5. Try to find a record of an actual debate or discussion which is reported in some detail. Judge it in terms of our description of the methods of limiting a discussion. Were both sides clear about what was to be proved? Were they agreed on what could constitute a proof? Were points or issues raised that were impossible to settle satisfactorily? If so, why?

CHAPTER 6
WEAK ARGUMENTS

Fallacious arguments give us no good reason to think that their conclusions are true. The arguments which we are now going to consider give us *some* reason to believe in their conclusions, but in most cases *not enough* reason. If we put more confidence in these weak arguments than they deserve, we will be misled. But if we treat them with care they can be useful.

AUTHORITY

Pretty obviously we accept a great number of things on the authority of other people. We know that George Washington was the first President of the United States, that Eskimos build igloos, that Jacqueline Kennedy married Aristotle Onassis, because other people have told us so. None of us were alive for Washington's inauguration, and few of us know about either the Eskimos or the Onassis family by personal experience. Of course we can, to some extent, check such accounts, but in many cases we find ourselves simply comparing other peoples' testimonies with the first account. Acceptance of authority in this very wide sense is one characteristic way of knowing about things. Some interesting questions can be asked about how we are justified in accepting such testimony, but for the purposes of this chapter we will talk about arguments from authority in a somewhat narrower sense. By an argument from authority we will mean the attempt to prove a conclusion true by appealing to the authority of an expert in some field. We often find such arguments in advertisements: "Nine out of ten doctors agree . . . ," "Scientists have shown . . . ," etc. The testimony of experts also has a recognized place in our legal system, and there are legal rules that settle such matters as when expert testimony is allowable, how much weight it is to be given, and so on.

In order to offer useful rules for deciding how much weight to give in everyday situations to arguments from the authority of experts, we will make use of the list of questions often used to remind young reporters of the essential points to put in a story: Who? What? Where? When? Why? We will give each of these our own interpretation, but it will be close enough to the usual one to be easily remembered.

1. *Who?* If an appeal is made to the authority of an expert, we must first know who the expert is. A device often used in advertising is the *faceless expert.* Dishonest copywriters use such phrases as "Doctors agree . . ." or "Scientists have shown . . ." without giving us any idea of which doctors or which scientists.

2. *What?* We must also know what the expert is an expert *on*, what qualifications he has. The opinion of "Dr. Smith" on the safety of the birth control pill may be of little value if he is a rural GP with little knowledge of the latest research. A full description of his qualifications gives us an opportunity to see if the expert is an expert on what we are asked to take his word for. If a famous foot specialist gives us advice on the care of our feet, we may do well to pay attention, but if he gives us advice on the care of our eyes or how to treat our wives, we may be less inclined to take his advice seriously.

3. *Where?* The geographical location of the expert, as well as the region to which his statement is intended to apply, can be important. An expert who has lived all his life in a tropical country may be unfamiliar with conditions outside the tropics, and his expertise may

not apply to conditions that he is not familiar with. Sometimes so-called experts on a given country may never have visited that country, or have visited it only briefly.

On some occasions such caution may be misplaced. During World War II, Ruth Benedict, an American anthropologist who had never visited Japan, made a study of Japanese culture based on available documents and information from informants. (Her study was later published under the title *Chrysanthemum and Sword*.) Many Japanese, and many people who had spent years in Japan, found Professor Benedict's study accurate and illuminating. But the combination of circumstances that made this feat possible does not occur often. Usually we would look with justifiable caution at an "expert" on Africa who had never been to Africa, an "expert" on urban poverty who had never visited a slum.

4. *When?* Again we can apply this question in two ways. How long ago the expert made his statement can be important, especially in fields where knowledge increases very rapidly. For example, Adam Smith was a great economist, but few of his opinions would be accepted without qualification by contemporary economists. Again, many statements made by experts are true enough for some limited period of time, but are mistakenly extended beyond these limits. An example is the mistaken attempt to continue to use, at a time when recession had begun, expert advice that applied to a period of inflation.

However, a frequently committed error on the other side is what is sometimes called *chronological snobbery*. It operates when expert testimony is discounted because it was given long ago, even though it is still applicable; or when useful advice is discarded because conditions have changed, although the advice may for other reasons still be applicable under the new conditions. An example of the first error would be to disregard the testimony of a shrewd observer of human nature, say Shakespeare or Dr. Johnson, just because he lived a long time ago. An example of the second error might be a teen-age athlete's decision to stop drinking milk because he feels he is not a kid any more, although his doctor's advice to drink plenty of milk, given a few years before, might still be valid.

5. *Why?* The motive for an expert's testimony may be important in judging the worth of that testimony. If an expert stands to gain financially or in other ways from making a certain statement, we must take this fact into account. An expert may have some axe to grind or be riding some personal hobbyhorse. For example, a historian who is a Marxist may overemphasize the economic aspect in a particular situation. An Irish historian may find the influence of Ireland in history somewhat greater than his colleagues consider justified by the facts, and so on. Of course, this sort of caution can be exaggerated. Since any expert is a human being he will have some interests, dislikes, or hobbies that may tempt him to distort the facts. This does not mean every expert is untrustworthy, only that we should exercise caution when there seems a clear motive for bias, and statements are made to fit that bias.

On the positive side, it may be well to say something about the standards by which we can tell when expert testimony is trustworthy. They parallel to some extent the negative standards we have just discussed.

1. A genuine expert will generally be known to others in his field, listed in reference books, associated with well-known institutions, etc.
2. Expert testimony should be dated and located geographically, and any limitations on its applicability should be noted.
3. An expert should be impartial, or at least frankly admit any reasons for partiality which he may have.

There are some obvious limitations on even the strongest argument from authority. The testimony of an expert cannot and should not convince us if we have personal experience to the contrary. For example, consider your reaction if an education expert stated that every teacher in your school was a brilliant teacher. We should not depend on experts where it is easy to find out the truth for ourselves either by personal experience or by reasoning or calculation. If an expert assured you that mixing sugar and salt in warm water caused the mixture to bubble furiously, or that every multiple of 9 is divisible by 5, it would be so easy to test these assertions that it would be foolish to trust to them merely on the word of the expert. On the other hand, we can also test true propositions. If the expert asserts that salt lowers the freezing temperature of water or that every multiple of 9 is divisible by 3, we can easily prove these things for ourselves and no longer have to rely on the expert's testimony .

There are also matters difficult to decide, of such great personal importance to the individual that most people are unwilling to trust to experts in making decisions. An obvious example for most people in our civilization is the choice of a spouse. The choice of a religious belief or unbelief and the choice of a standard of morality are other examples of choices of great personal importance. Some people seem content to leave such choices to those they regard as experts. Others wish to make such choices for themselves or at least to be very sure of the credibility of the authority they trust in such matters.

In conclusion, we can say that some arguments from the authority of experts should be taken seriously, but that all such arguments should be given a critical examination, in some cases a much more critical examination than they in fact receive.

ANALOGY

Another useful but sometimes dangerous argument is the argument from analogy. We see that X is like Y in many respects—a, b, c, . . . , etc.—and we see that Y has property p. We then conclude that X also has property p. This is a type of argument which people do in fact use. For example if your car is like mine in make, model, year, etc., and mine is hard to start on cold mornings, I may guess that your car is also hard to start on cold mornings. If you and I have similar tastes in books, friends, life-style, etc., and I enjoyed a certain vacation spot, I may conclude that you would also enjoy it. Many guesses, hunches and estimates are based on analogies, and many of these prove true in fact.

But analogy may prove treacherous. My car's starting difficulties may be due to a defective switch and not be characteristic of cars of that make and model. While your tastes and mine may be similar in many ways, our tastes in climate or sports may produce a taste in widely differing vacation spots.

Also, it is true that not every similarity between things leads us to suppose further similarities. College professors may have certain interests or characteristics in common, but brown-haired people may be unlike in everything but their hair. All 1960 Fords may have some characteristics in common but white cars may vary in all sorts of ways, being alike only in color. Thus it would seem to be true that we must confine ourselves in some ways to *relevant* characteristics of X and Y if any argument from analogy is to work at all. But how are we to be sure that certain similarities between X and Y are relevant to the possession of property *p* by X?

One way of approaching this problem is to look for what I will call the *maxim* of a given analogy. In trying to state the maxim we are often able to see whether or not certain similar characteristics are relevant to the possession of some further characteristic. We might state the maxim of our car example as follows:

Cars of similar make, model, and year often have
similar mechanical problems.

We then add the information

Our cars are of similar make, model, and year, and
mine has a starting problem.

We can then conclude with some plausibility

Your car is likely to have a starting problem.

On the other hand the maxim

Cars of similar color, with the same number of windows, and with similar upholstery, have similar mechanical problems.

is extremely implausible, and we are not likely to add

Our cars are of similar color, have the same number of windows, and have similar upholstery, and mine has a starting problem.

and conclude that

Your car is likely to have a starting problem.

Notice that even if the maxim is extremely plausible the only conclusion we can reasonably reach is that the conclusion is likely or probable; it *may* be true. If the maxim is strong enough to justify a positive conclusion, we no longer have an argument from analogy but a *deductive* argument (this kind of argument will be discussed in the next section). Thus

Every chemical characteristic of one sample of gold is a chemical characteristic of every sample of gold. My sample of gold has the chemical characteristic of not being soluble in citric acid. Therefore your sample of gold has the chemical characteristic of not being soluble in citric acid.

is not an analogy argument at all, but a deductive argument.

Sometimes an analogy between two situations can give us valuable information even though the two situations are different in almost every respect. A clever piano mover had the idea of making a rough mock-up out of cardboard and scrap wood of each piano he was asked to move. This mock-up, of course, could not be played, did not look very much like the piano, and so on. But it had the same dimensions as the real piano. The mover and his assistants would then make a trial run with the mock-up, moving it through the doors and corridors and up the stairs along the route on which the real piano was to be moved. If the mock-up got stuck at any point, he knew that the real piano could not be moved along that route. (Mock-ups of new cars and airplanes that are tested in a wind tunnel make use of the same idea.)

Analogies can also be used in teaching when we use familiar examples to put across new principles, as in the parables of Christ. Analogies can be used negatively to show that a rule or principle which seems innocent in one case is obviously dangerous or silly when applied to an analogous case. A positive use of the same technique is to make a principle which applies to one case more understandable by citing an analogous but more familiar case to which it also applies.

One other use of analogy ought to be mentioned before we leave the subject. An analogy that is far from giving a conclusive reason for believing something may offer a hypothesis that is worth entertaining. If the starting trouble on my 1967 Dodge was due to a sticking valve on the carburetor, and your 1966 Chrysler is having trouble, checking the same valve may be worthwhile. If light seems to behave in certain respects like waves in water, and we know that waves in water can reinforce or interfere with each other, we might look for interference and reinforcement phenomena in light. (The verification of such suggestions in fact led scientists to adopt a wave theory of light at the time of Newton and Huygens.)

ABDUCTION

Abduction is a word used by C. S. Peirce, the great American philosopher and logician, to mean the "method of hypothesis," which Peirce identified as the method of science. He thought of abduction as different from both deduction and induction. But Peirce's use of the term was never generally adopted. We shall use the term to designate a weak form of argument related to scientific method, that is in some respects similar to Peirce's method of hypothesis. Let me give an example of this kind of argument. I observe one of my friends coming to work one morning with red eyes. He blows his nose violently, then goes to a water fountain and takes a small capsule with a drink of water. Since my friend has suffered from hay fever in the past, I conclude that he is having another such attack. The form of the argument I have used is something like this:

Observed facts: Red eyes, nose blowing, taking a capsule similar to those used for hay fever remedies.

Background information: Previous hay fever attacks. Hypothesis which accounts for observed facts and fits background information: If my friend has hay fever, the known facts would be accounted for. Conclusion: My friend does in fact have hay fever.

But this is not the end of the story. Shortly afterward my friend leaves the building. I comment to someone that it must be a very severe hay fever attack he is having. The man stares at me. "Didn't you know?" he says. "His family was killed in a fire last night. He just came in to pick up some things before going on sick leave. He's all to pieces—been taking tranquilizers steadily since it happened." The lesson of this story is that not every hypothesis that fits the known facts is true.

Abduction, or the method of hypothesis, can be characterized as forming a hypothesis that apparently accounts for the facts and accepting it without further investigation. Often we jump to the conclusion that some hypothesis that apparently accounts for the facts *is* true. As we shall see in the next section, one form of scientific method, the hypothetico-deductive method, resembles abduction in some respects. And in fact there is nothing wrong with forming hypotheses in an attempt to account for facts. What is mistaken in abduction is the failure to consider other possible hypotheses, to look for evidence that will confirm or disconfirm a proposed hypothesis, and so on. It is the *uncritical* acceptance of hypotheses that is being criticized.

We see the result of relying on the abductive type of argument in many people who are quick to form hypotheses, but slow to subject them to any criticism or test. Their curiosity is quickly aroused and quickly satisfied. Once they have abduced a hypothesis that seems to account for the facts, they lose interest in the problem. Human vanity plays a part here. If someone is asked "Why do you think those men are digging a hole in the road there?", very few people are strong-minded enough to reply simply "I don't know" or "I haven't a clue." We spin some hypothesis, and once we have put it forth our interest and that of our questioner is satisfied. Perhaps this is not even a clear-cut case of abduction, since neither party seriously believes the proposed explanation.

However, people use essentially the same method in much more serious matters. Looking at the complex problems of the world, they tend to seek simple explanations for such events. If the Communist conspiracy, or the capitalist conspiracy, or the machinations of the Pope, the Jews, the blacks, the whites, the Chinese, or whatever they may choose as their villain seems to explain the events which trouble them, they accept the explanation uncritically and subject it to no further criticism.

Another manifestation of the same tendency is the way in which some people seem to believe that finding an alternative explanation for some state of affairs amounts to refuting the original explanation. Comparing the two explanations and judging their relative merits never seem to occur to them. For example, they feel they have disproved the existence of God if they put forward the hypothesis that the idea of God is the result of *projection* (as in Freudian theories) or of unfulfilled economic needs (as in Marxist theories). The existence or nonexistence of God is an important and difficult question, but merely finding a possible alternate explanation of some men's idea of God does little to answer it. Such arguments prove too little, for precisely similar arguments could be given on the other side (for example that the denial of God's existence is a projected oedipal longing to destroy the father). Such arguments also prove too much, since any reality which was felt to be reassuring or desirable (for example Social Security or the United Nations) could be attacked on the same grounds.

Thus in subjecting an abductive argument to test and criticism, we begin to approach the methods of science. But so long as the method of hypothesis remains *only* a method of hypothesis, without test or criticism, it is a weak form of argument, dangerous if trusted too far. This warning applies to all the weak arguments we have considered: All have something to be said in their favor, none is completely trustworthy.

CASES

How impressive would you find the opinions of the following authorities on the following subjects? What doubts or reservations would you have about their reliability? What further information would you like to have to help you make a judgment?

1. Neil Armstrong on lunar exploration.
2. Neil Armstrong on undersea exploration.
3. The Pope on Catholic doctrines.
4. The Pope on world population problems.
5. The President of the United States on the domestic political scene.
6. The President of the United States on world population problems.
7. The winner of the last Nobel Prize in physics on space exploration.
8. The winner of the last Nobel Prize in physics on the existence of God.
9. The author of this book on logic.
10. The author of this book on space exploration, undersea exploration, Catholic doctrine, world population problems, the domestic political scene, or the existence of God.

Treat the following brief comparisons as analogies. Try to find the maxim of the analogy. What properties do the things or situations have in common? Which of these are relevant?

11. The modern world is like a hijacked airliner.
12. Life, said Pythagoras, is like a fair, some come to compete, some to buy or sell, but the best people come as spectators.
13. The Kingdom of Heaven is like a grain of mustard seed.
14. The Kingdom of Heaven is like a treasure hidden in a field: The man who found it went and sold everything he had to buy the field.

15. It is no matter what you teach children first, any more than what leg you put into your breeches first. You may stand disputing which is best to put in first, but in the meantime your breech is bare. While you are considering which of two things you should teach your child first, another boy has learnt them both (From Boswell's *Life of Johnson*).

Invent at least two incompatible hypotheses to account for each of the following phenomena. In each case suggest a possible way of deciding between the hypotheses.

16. The rise and fall of women's skirts.

17. The rise of Women's Liberation movements.

18. The increasing use of drugs by young people.

19. The failure of people to use public transportation in many large cities.

20. Changes in forms of worship and doctrines in many Christian churches.

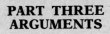

PART THREE
ARGUMENTS

To arrive at decisions on the basis of evidence, we need not only to be clear and critical, but also to know something about good argumentation. There are two main types of reasoning: deduction and induction. Deductive reasoning involves arguments whose conclusion must be true if their premises are true, while inductive reasoning involves arguments whose conclusion is given a certain degree of probability if their premises are true. In the two chapters devoted to deductive logic, we consider first simple propositional arguments and then more complex arguments involving the distinction between all and some. In the two chapters on inductive reasoning we look first at the making of generalizations, especially generalizations that state causal relations. We then consider more complex problems having to do with scientific and statistical methods and the relation of science to common sense. This section should enable you to recognize and criticize the common types of deductive and inductive arguments and also to construct your own deductive and inductive arguments.

CHAPTER 7
DEDUCTION I

In the preceding chapters we have talked about some preliminaries and preconditions of agreement—for example agreement about terms—and some weak or inadequate arguments. In this chapter we will begin the positive approach to argument. Negative criticism of arguments is important, but the ability to recognize and originate good arguments is even more important. Rules and directions cannot make up for a complete lack of originality and reasoning ability, but most people have at least a modicum of this ability, and in this chapter we will begin trying to improve your powers of reasoning.

PROPOSITIONS AND THEIR RELATIONS

At least in the more basic forms of logic we have to confine ourselves to statements which are definitely true or definitely false. Questions, commands, requests, etc., as well as statements that are too vague, confused, or paradoxical to have a definite truth value have to be left out of consideration. We will use the term *proposition* to refer to this somewhat restricted class of statements (those which are definitely true or definitely false) and talk henceforth only about propositions. This simplifies our task considerably without leaving out anything essential to the study of arguments, at least at the basic level.

Another simplification we will introduce is the assumption that we can always state the exact opposite or *contradictory* of any proposition: the proposition which is false if the original proposition is true and true if the original proposition is false. There are many ways of forming the contradictory of a proposition in ordinary language, but we can always get the contradictory of a proposition by putting some such phrase as *it is not true that* or *it is false that* in front of the original proposition.

It will sometimes be convenient to let single letters stand for a whole proposition, especially where we want to make general statements that apply to any proposition. Thus part of the paragraph above could be rewritten as: "For any proposition *A*, we can get the contradictory of *A* by putting the phrase *it is not true that* or *it is false that* in front of *A*, so *it is false that A* is the contradictory of *A*. Actually, it will often be convenient to abbreviate further. Instead of writing out *"it is false that A"* we will simply write *not A*, which will be shorthand for any contradictory of *A*. Thus if *A* were "Alaska is the forty-ninth state," then *not A* would stand for "It is false that Alaska is the forty-ninth state," or "Alaska is not the forty-ninth state," or any proposition that means the same as these propositions.

The simplest propositions have one subject and one predicate, but some propositions with more than one subject, for example "Alaska is larger than Texas" cannot really be broken up into simpler propositions, and will be regarded for our purposes as *simple* propositions. The rule which we will use to tell whether a proposition is a simple one is this: We will regard a proposition as a simple one if it cannot be restated as two simpler propositions which have the same meaning as the original. Thus for example, "Alaska and Texas have salt-water ports" can be restated as "Alaska has salt-water ports" and "Texas has salt-water ports." But there is no way of restating "Alaska is larger than

Texas" as two simpler propositions which have the same meaning as the original proposition.

Simple propositions can be combined into compound propositions by the use of words like *and, or, if,* and so on. Thus, from the two propositions "Alaska is the largest state" and "Alaska is larger than Colorado" we can form the compound propositions "Alaska is the largest state and Alaska is larger than Colorado," "Alaska is the largest state or Alaska is larger than Colorado," "If Alaska is the largest state, Alaska is larger than Colorado." These statements might also be expressed as "Alaska is *both* the largest state and larger than Colorado," *"Either* Alaska is the largest state or Alaska is larger than Colorado," and "If Alaska is the largest state *then* Alaska is larger than Colorado." Words like *both, either,* and *then* help to group compound statements, as we will see.

It is sometimes necessary to express the idea that if a proposition *A* is true then some other proposition *B* is true and vice versa—that is, if *B* is true *A* is true. We use expressions like *if and only if* or *just in case* to express this double idea, for example "Alaska is the largest state if and only if it is larger than Texas" or "Alaska is the largest state just in case Alaska is larger than Texas." Notice that such a statement can be restated as two *if* statements: "If Alaska is larger than Texas then Alaska is the largest state" and "If Alaska is the largest state then Alaska is larger than Texas."

Other complications have to do with *or* and *and.* The complication which has to do with *or* is that sometimes *"A or B"* means *"A or B* and maybe both," and sometimes it means *"A or B* and definitely not both." "Alaska is the largest state or Hawaii is the smallest state (or maybe both)" is an example of the first, while "Alaska is the largest state or Texas is the largest state" is an example of the second.

The complication about *and* is that sometimes we use *and* to do extra work, using it to mean *and then* or *and therefore;* for example "Alaska became a state and (then) Hawaii became a state" and "Alaska is the largest state and (therefore) Texas is not the largest state." Since in logic we want to take nothing for granted we will always take the weakest and most general possible meaning of *or* and *and.* Thus unless we explicitly state otherwise *"A* or *B"* will always be interpreted as *"A* or *B* and maybe both," and *"A* and *B"* will never mean *"A* and then *B"* or *"A* and therefore *B."*

Notice that as we have defined *simple statement,* the contradictory of a simple statement is a simple statement. We can think of this in a different way, since we get the contradictory of a simple statement by adding an identifiable expression like *not* or *it is false that* to an original statement. For our purposes, however, we will regard the contradictory of a simple statement as simple, and the contradictory of a compound statement as compound. Notice how the grouping words *both, either,* and *then* help avoid ambiguity when we mix negative ideas with compounds. Thus "It is not true that Alaska is the largest state and Hawaii is the smallest state" might mean either "It is not true both that Alaska is the largest state and that Hawaii is the smallest" or it might mean "Alaska is *not* the largest state and Hawaii *is* the smallest." The first of the statements could be true and the second false, so they are obviously not the same. Similarly, "Either Alaska is not the largest state or Hawaii is not the smallest" is different from "It is not true either that Alaska is the largest state or that Hawaii is the smallest" but either could be meant by "It is not true that Alaska is the largest state or Hawaii is the smallest."

Finally, notice all the variations we can get in an *if* statement by moving the position of the negative: "It is false that if Alaska is the largest state then Texas is the smallest," "If it is false that Alaska is the largest state then Texas is the smallest," "If Alaska is the largest state, then Texas is not the smallest."

There are further complications but most of them can be taken up as we come to them in the following discussion of arguments.

PROPOSITIONAL ARGUMENTS AND FALLACIES

In this section we will learn to recognize certain common patterns of good argument and the "look-alike" bad arguments that are often confused with them. We will show the goodness or badness of arguments by giving examples which make their logic as obvious as possible. We will first state each good argument and its bad twin in shorthand form using letters to stand for propositions, then discuss each of the "twins." In naming arguments we will use the Greek word *syllogism*, which basically means any argument with two premises and one conclusion. (A premise, as you should be aware, is a statement that is offered in support or as proof of a conclusion.)

Another bit of useful terminology has to do with *if* propositions. Such propositions are called *conditionals* or *conditional propositions*, since they say one is true on condition that something else is true. The first simple statement in a conditional is called the *antecedent*, the second is called the *consequent*. It is also a good idea to remember that a conditional can be expressed in a variety of ways. "If *A*, *B*" "If *A* then *B*" "*B* if *A*" "*A* only if *B*" are all equivalent ways of saying the same thing.

This first argument we will consider is called *Conditional Syllogism*. You may sometimes find it referred to by its Latin name, *modus ponens*, but we will try to avoid using technical terms that are not in English and have to be memorized by rote. It has this general form:

$$\text{If } A \text{ then } B$$
$$\underline{A}$$
$$B$$

Notice that we divide the premises "If A then B" and "A," from the conclusion "B" by a line like that in an arithmetic problem, suggesting that the premises add up to the conclusion. An example of this general type of argument is the following:

If Alaska is the largest state then Texas is not the
                                largest state.
Alaska is the largest state.
_____
Texas is not the largest state.

We can see that this particular argument is a good one, but how can we be sure that any argument of this general pattern will be a good one? We mean by a good argument that if the premises are true then the conclusion must be true. Does the pattern of argument we have just looked at meet this standard?

To see that it does, consider the following geographical version of the argument:

If you are in the United States you are in North America.

You are in the United States.

You are in North America.

Let us draw a schematic diagram of this argument:

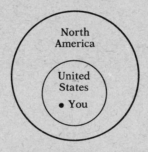

Now if the first premise is true, the circle representing the United States must be inside the North America circle. If the second premise is true, the dot representing you must be drawn inside the United States. But then it follows necessarily that the dot representing you must be in the North America circle—there is no escaping it.

Of course either premise could be false. You might be reading this in Australia, in which case the second premise is false. The first premise actually is false, since if you are in Hawaii you are in the United States, but not in North America. But if both premises were true, the conclusion would have to be true, and this is what we mean by calling an argument a good one.

Logic can only guarantee that *if* you start off with true
information and use good arguments, you will get true
conclusions. Establishing the truth of the premises is
up to science, history, philosophy, or whatever field of
study is appropriate in a given case.

The name we have given to the pattern of argument
we have just been discussing is Conditional Syllogism.

The counterfeit argument which is very much like
Conditional Syllogism is the following:

$$\frac{\text{If } A \text{ then } B}{A}$$

It is called the *Fallacy of Affirming the Consequent*,
since its difference from Conditional Syllogism is that
the consequent of the conditional, rather than its antecedent, is affirmed as the second premise. An example of this fallacy is the following:

If you are in Canada you are in North America.
You are in North America.

You are in Canada.

Now something is obviously wrong, since both the
premises can be true and the conclusion false. In terms
of our diagram the situation is this:

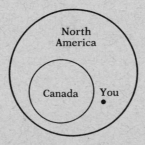

You can easily be in North America—in the United
States or Mexico—without being in Canada. You *could*

be in North America and also in Canada, but being in North America does not *guarantee* that you are in Canada. That the conclusion *may* be true when the premises are true is not enough to make the argument a good one; for a good argument the conclusion *must* be true if the premises are. But because the Fallacy of Affirming the Consequent looks rather like the good argument that we have called Conditional Syllogism, many people are taken in by the fallacy, especially in cases where the conclusion is not blatantly or obviously false.

The second argument that we will consider we will call *Negative Conditional Syllogism*. It is also known by the Latin name *modus tollens*. It has the general form:

> If *A* then *B*
> Not *B*
> _____
> Not *A*

Here is an example of this argument:

If Texas is the largest state, then Texas would have the largest area.
Texas does not have the largest area.
_____
Texas is not the largest state.

We will regard any case where the opposite of the consequent of a conditional is asserted in order to deny the antecedent of that conditional as a case of Negative Conditional Syllogism. Thus the following argument

If Texas is the largest state then Alaska is not the largest state.
Alaska is the largest state.
_____
Texas is not the largest state.

is an example of Negative Conditional Syllogism, because even though the second premise is positive, it is the contradictory of the consequent of the conditional.

We can see that this argument is a good one by considering the following geographical version of the argument.

If you are in Brazil, you are in South America.
You are not in South America.

* You are not in Brazil.

To use a diagram like the one we used for the last argument:

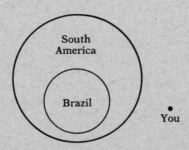

We can see that if we draw the dot representing you outside the South America circle, then there is no possible way in which it can be inside the Brazil circle. Again, either premise could be false, but if both are true the conclusion must be true.

The fallacy which resembles this argument is called the *Fallacy of Denying the Antecedent* and it has this form:

If *A* then *B*
Not *A*

Not *B*

Here is an example:

If Alaska is warm, then Brazil is tropical.
Alaska is not warm.

Brazil is not tropical.

It is like the geographical argument,

If you are in Canada then you are in North America.
You are not in Canada.

You are not in North America.

We can diagram it as follows.

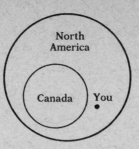

It is apparent that both premises can be true and the conclusion false (for example you could be in Texas, therefore in North America). Thus the argument cannot be a good one, since some examples of it can have true premises and a false conclusion.

The next argument is called *Disjunctive Syllogism* (*disjunction* is a logician's word for a compound statement connected with an *or*). It has this form:

$$
\begin{array}{l}
\text{Either } A \text{ or } B \\
\underline{\text{Not } A} \\
B
\end{array}
$$

Here is an example:

Either you are in the Southern Hemisphere or you are
in the Northern Hemisphere.
You are not in the Southern Hemisphere.
_____

You are in the Northern Hemisphere.

We can diagram it like this:

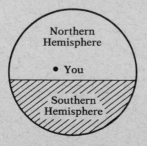

The shading in the Southern Hemisphere indicates that what we are concerned with, you in this case, is not in the Southern Hemisphere; in other words the Southern Hemisphere is "empty" of you. Thus, since we must put you either in the Northern Hemisphere or the Southern Hemisphere we are forced to put you in the Northern Hemisphere. The premises could be false—for example an astronaut in space is in neither hemisphere —but if they are true the conclusion must be true.

The fallacy that we will call *False Disjunctive Syllogism* has the form:

Either A or B
A
_____
Not B

Here is an example:

Either you are in the United States or you are in North America.
You are in the United States.
_____
You are not in North America.

The trouble of course is that you can be *both* in the United States and in North America. Remember that we will always interpret "A or B" as meaning "one or the other and maybe both." So unless we are sure that "one or the other and *not* both" is meant we must assume that both A and B are possible; thus merely because A is true, it does not follow that B is false.

When we are sure that two propositions cannot both be true we have the following good argument, which we will call *Conjunctive Syllogism* (a conjunction is an *and* statement):

Not both A and B
A
_____
Not B

For example:

It is not true both that you are in the United States and that you are in Brazil.
You are in the United States.
_____
You are not in Brazil.

We can diagram it as follows:

We can see that if Brazil and the United States do not overlap, and you are in the United States, you cannot be in Brazil. Similarly, whenever two statements cannot both be true, then if one is true the other must be false.

The fallacy that resembles this argument we will call *False Conjunctive Syllogism*.

It has the form:

Not both *A* and *B*
Not *A*
_____
B

For example:

It is not true both that you are in Argentina and that you are in Brazil.
You are not in Argentina.
_____
You are in Brazil.

The catch here is that you could be *neither* in Argentina nor in Brazil. And in general, whenever two statements cannot both be true, then if one is false the other may be false also.

The final argument we will consider is called *Hypothetical Syllogism*. It has the form:

If *A* then *B*
If *B* then *C*
_____
If *A* then *C*

For example:

If you are in Canada you are in North America.
If you are in North America you are in the Northern
Hemisphere.

If you are in Canada you are in the Northern Hemisphere.

We can diagram it as follows:

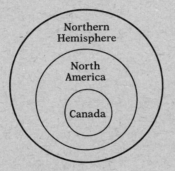

Obviously there is no way to put the dot representing
you in the Canada circle without also putting it inside
the Northern Hemisphere circle. But notice that we
have not reached a definite, unconditional assertion
as the conclusion of our argument; we have merely
reached a conditional conclusion on the basis of two
other conditionals. This is why the argument is called
Hypothetical Syllogism.

The matching fallacy we will call *False Hypothetical
Syllogism*. It has this form:

If *A* then *B*
If *C* then *B*

If *A* then *C*

For example:

If you are in the United States then you are in North
America.
If you are in Canada then you are in North America.

If you are in the United States then you are in Canada.

A diagram looks like the following.

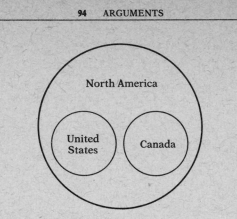

But of course the fact that two areas are included in another does not mean they are included within each other; and, in general, the fact that two antecedents have the same consequent does not mean that one is the consequent of the other.

We could describe other common argument patterns and fallacies but these are the most frequently encountered. We will now see how we can analyze complex arguments by using the simple patterns described so far.

PUTTING TOGETHER AND TAKING APART ARGUMENTS
The list of arguments given in the last section is actually quite a short one. You may wonder how we can analyze very many arguments with such simple machinery. There are two answers to this; the first is that these arguments appear over and over again in real disputes and discussions. The second answer is that we can put together more complex arguments using the simple arguments as parts, and that some complex arguments we encounter in real situations can be taken apart again into simple arguments like the ones we have given.

For example consider the following argument:

If you have been to Calgary, you have been to Alberta. If you have been to Alberta, you have been to Canada. You have never been to Canada.

You have never been to Calgary.

Set up in this way it is easy enough to see that from
the first two premises it follows by Hypothetical Syllogism that

If you have been to Calgary you have been to Canada.

And this statement, together with the final premise,
gives you the conclusion indicated above, by Negative
Conditional Syllogism. However, you might find this
argument stated much more informally in a real conversation or discussion. For example
    "You know you've never been to Calgary, Sam. I
don't know why you're unsure about it. Calgary is in
Alberta, and Alberta is part of Canada, and you've
never been out of the United States in your life."
Faced with a real argument of this kind we have not
only to untangle the various simple arguments being
used, but also to tidy up the argument a bit and supply some missing pieces. In this version of the argument we have not said just "You have never been in
Canada" but rather "You have never been out of the
United States." If we want to be very careful we
might regard this as an additional subargument:

If you have never been out of the United States you
                        have never been in Canada.
You have never been out of the United States.

You have never been in Canada.

It may seem overcautious to state this as a subargument but sometimes such seemingly obvious moves
can cause trouble. Consider the following argument:
    "Of course you've never been to Waimea, Harry. It's
on an island called Kauai, and you told me you've
never been outside the United States." Harry can perfectly well reply "Kauai is one of the Hawaiian Islands,
and Hawaii is one of the United States; I was there on
vacation last year." One of the advantages of putting
down an argument in a formal way is that it forces
you to put down each premise of the argument and
think about its justification. In this case the premise
"If you are on the island of Kauai you are not in the
United States" turns out not to be true.

There is no simple rule of thumb for dealing with complex arguments, but very often you can do something like the following: First set down the argument as clearly as you can, in the form of premises and conclusion. Then look for some pair of premises from which you can derive a conclusion, using one of the simple forms of argument. Then take that conclusion and see if you can put it together with one of the remaining original premises to reach a new conclusion. If everything goes well, you should be able to arrive at the original conclusion of the complex argument after having used all of the original premises, together with subconclusions you have drawn using simple arguments.

Of course real arguments, as opposed to examples in logic books, are not always neat and tidy. If you are able to get the original conclusion without using all of the original premises, it may mean that the original argument had *excess* premises that were not needed to prove the conclusion. You may need to supply some obviously missing premise, as in the example we gave. Very often you will need to put the argument in such a way that the connections are made obvious enough so that the simple argument forms can be used. In the informal version of the Calgary argument it was necessary to put together such premises as *"You* have never been in Canada" with such premises as *"Calgary* is in Alberta," which has a different subject. We did this by rewriting "Calgary is in Alberta" as "If you are in Calgary, you are in Alberta." Such rewriting of statements to get the argument to fit conveniently into our standard patterns of argument is often necessary. Of course not every rewriting is acceptable, only those that preserve the meaning of the original.

In doing any of the things that are necessary for laying out an argument in a formal way, a certain amount of ingenuity is necessary. No set rules can be given to insure success, so setting up the argument formally is often the hardest part of analyzing it. But this is true in other fields too. For instance, once the time-consuming task of setting up a computer program for a problem has been accomplished, the computer can solve the problem in a few minutes.

Since no rules can be given, the best way to acquire skill at putting arguments together and taking them apart is practice. You should work as many as possible of the problems at the end of this chapter.

CASES

Identify the pattern of the following arguments. Are they valid or invalid? Some of the invalid arguments sound plausible. Explain briefly why the conclusion does not follow from the premises.

1. If Charley Brown misses this ball, he'll be the goat. Of course he'll be the goat, so he'll miss the ball.

2. Either Linus will see the Great Pumpkin, or he'll wait in the pumpkin patch all night. He won't see the Great Pumpkin, so he'll wait in the pumpkin patch all night.

3. It's not true that both Linus and Sally will see the Great Pumpkin. Linus won't see the Great Pumpkin, so Sally will.

4. If Charley Brown tries to steal home, he'll lose the game. He'll try to steal home, so he'll lose the game.

5. If Charley Brown had the nerve, he'd speak to the little red-haired girl. He won't speak to her, so he doesn't have the nerve.

6. Either Snoopy or the Red Baron will be shot down. Snoopy will be shot down, so the Red Baron won't be.

7. Snoopy and the Red Baron won't both be shot down. Snoopy will be, so the Red Baron won't be.

8. If Lucy married Schroeder, she'd have to admire Beethoven. If Lucy appreciated good music, she'd admire Beethoven. So if Lucy married Schroeder, she'd appreciate good music.

9. If Lucy is grouchy, someone will get yelled at. Lucy isn't grouchy, so no one will get yelled at.

10. If Charley Brown chooses a Christmas tree, Lucy won't like it. If Lucy doesn't like it, the others will laugh at Charley Brown. So if Charley Brown chooses a Christmas tree, the others will laugh at him.

Break down the following arguments into simple arguments and identify them. Is the argument as a whole valid or invalid? If the argument is invalid, explain why.

11. If Snoopy causes any more trouble, he'll be sent to Daisy Hill Puppy Farm. If he is sent there, he'll stop at Peppermint Pattie's house. Snoopy has stopped at Peppermint Pattie's house, so he has caused more trouble.

12. If Sally waits in the pumpkin patch, Charley Brown will have to ask for extra treats when he goes trick-or-treating. Either Sally waits in the pumpkin patch or she doesn't believe in the Great Pumpkin. Charley Brown doesn't have to ask for extra treats. So Sally doesn't believe in the Great Pumpkin.

13. If Snoopy won the World Wrist-Wrestling Championship, he would have to go to Petaluma. If he goes to Petaluma, he would pass Peppermint Pattie's house. Snoopy didn't win the World Wrist-Wrestling Championship. So Snoopy didn't pass Peppermint Pattie's house.

14. Snoopy cannot both have the Christmas spirit and keep his flashily decorated doghouse. If he refuses to give Charley Brown the ornaments on his doghouse for Charley Brown's tree, he will keep his flashily decorated doghouse. He does have Christmas spirit, so he won't refuse to give Charley Brown the ornaments.

15. If Charley Brown's team has girls or dogs on it, it can't get uniforms. Either Charley Brown's team has girls and dogs on it or he lets down his friends. He can't both let down his friends and keep his self-respect. Charley Brown will keep his self-respect, so his team won't get uniforms.

16. In your outside reading try to find and identify some of the forms of argument discussed in this chapter. Can you detect any invalid arguments that are examples of invalid forms we have discussed?

CHAPTER 8
DEDUCTION II

STATEMENTS

The argument forms we talked about in the last chapter, useful as they are, do not make an important distinction on which many arguments depend. This is the distinction between all and some. "Scots are thrifty, Sandy is a Scot, so Sandy is thrifty" is a good argument only if *all* Scots are thrifty. If only some are, then Sandy may be one of those who are not. Many arguments depend on this sort of distinction, so we must go a little deeper into deductive logic to be able to judge them.

Logicians have discovered that one way to handle arguments of this kind is to make all of our statements fit into a few simple patterns. Once we learn the rules that apply to these patterns, we will be able to deal with a surprisingly large number of arguments. These patterns, which are called *standard form statements,* are based on the distinction between all and some, positive and negative, and general terms and specific individuals. Each standard form statement has a single subject and a single predicate, but these may be quite complex.

The simplest cases are those where we make a statement about a specific individual. We can say that

Sandy is a Scot, or that Sandy is not a Scot. We can say that Sandy is or is not a dour, thrifty, whisky-drinking Scot. Of course no all or some distinction applies to individuals, and the subject is always a specific, named person or thing; no matter how complex the predicate, the subject is always simple. Our standard form statements do not permit multiple subjects in statements about individuals; "Sandy and Angus are Scots" is not a standard form statement. Nor can the name of an individual be the predicate of a standard form statement; "Sandy is not Angus" is not a standard form statement. Theoretically, *is* or *is not* should stand between the subject and predicate; for example "Sandy is a whisky drinker" instead of "Sandy drinks whisky." This device often helps us to see just what the predicate term is and will help us to apply certain rules. But since this form is sometimes stilted and unnatural, we may express statements more loosely and naturally: "Sandy is dour" instead of "Sandy is a dour man."

Thus our first two standard form statements are either positive or negative statements about individuals, having one of the two forms:

(Name of individual) is (predicate).
(Name of individual) is not (predicate).

A convenient shorthand way of writing these forms is

N is P
N is not P

where N stands for the name of an individual and P for the predicate.

When our subject is a group of individuals, or even one individual spoken of in a general way, the all–some distinction becomes important. Thus, if I say "Scots are thrifty" I may mean every single Scot or only some. I can make either positive or negative statements about every single Scot, and thus our next two standard form statements are

Every (subject term) is (predicate).
No (subject term) is (predicate).

or in shorthand:

> Every *S* is *P*
> No *S* is *P*

Ordinary usage may substitute *all* for *every* and may use either a singular or a plural form with *no*. We can say

> Every Scot is thrifty.   or
> All Scots are thrifty.

and

> No Scot is extravagant.   or
> No Scots are extravagant.

We will prefer the *every* form and the singular with *no*, partly because it saves changing back and forth from singular to plural in an argument like "All Scots *are* thrifty, Sandy *is* a Scot, so Sandy *is* thrifty." But we are going to have somewhat stilted and unnatural forms no matter what choice we make, and we will have to get used to seeing the *all* and the plural with *no* in many arguments. When we encounter such arguments, we will either have to translate them into our standard form or treat them as if they had been translated in accordance with our rules.

A similar difficulty arises with the next two standard form statements:

> Some (subject term) is (predicate).
> Some (subject term) is not (predicate).

or in shorthand:

> Some *S* is *P*
> Some *S* is not *P*

These forms have a drawback: often the plural form, "Some Scots are whisky drinkers" rather than "Some Scot is a whisky drinker" is more natural. The advantage, however, is that sometimes we have information that justifies us in saying that *at least one* member of a group, perhaps more but perhaps not, has a certain characteristic. For example, we all know that at least one New Zealander, Sir Edmund Hillary, was on the

successful Everest expedition. We may not be sure
if some of his countrymen were on the expedition with
him, but we can say *"Some* New Zealander is one of
the men on the successful Everest expedition."* There
are many cases where all we mean by *some* is *at least
one,* and logicians cautiously prefer to use this meaning of *some,* just as they prefer to use the weaker
meaning of *or.*

Some variant forms occurring in ordinary usage
should be mentioned. *Only* as in "Only Scots eat haggis" can be puzzling, since what we mean by this is
"Every person who eats haggis is a Scot." We have to
switch the subject and predicate terms as well as replace the *only. Nothing but* and *all except* are even
trickier. "Angus drinks nothing but whisky" has to be
put into standard form as "Every drink which Angus
drinks is whisky," while "Sandy drinks everything except water" becomes *two* statements "No drink that
Sandy drinks is water" and "Every drink that is not
water is drunk by Sandy."

It is important to notice that in two standard form
statements, and *only* two, the subject and predicate
can be switched without changing the meaning. "No
Scot is extravagant" and "No extravagant person is a
Scot" mean the same, and so do "Some Scot is a whisky
drinker" and "Some whisky drinker is a Scot." But
"Every Scot is thrifty" does not mean the same as
"Every thrifty person is a Scot" nor, to take a more
striking example, does "Some woman is not a wife"
mean the same as "Some wife is not a woman." Re-
versing subject and predicate in statements about
individuals is sometimes permissible as long as we
follow our rule that the name of an individual may
not be a predicate.

Every . . . is and *Some . . . is* can have another form.
"Every person who is not thrifty is not a Scot" means
the same as "Every Scot is thrifty," and "Some person
who is not extravagant is not a non-Scot" means the
same as "Some Scot is not extravagant." But no one
but a logician would use a complicated form like
"Some person who is not extravagant is not a non-
Scot." One warning: "Not every Scot drinks whisky"

is equivalent to "Some Scot is not a whisky drinker"
and is *not* equivalent to "No Scot is a whisky drinker."
There are a few other equivalences which are sometimes useful. "Every wife is a woman" means the same
as "No nonwoman is a wife," and "No man is a mother"
means the same as "Every man is a nonmother." But
"Every wife is not happy" or "Not every wife is happy"
is equivalent to "Some wife is not happy" rather than
to "No wife is happy." Often, however, faced with a
variant form of statement, we simply have to try the
subject and predicate in various standard form statements, and use our common sense and knowledge of
English until we find an equivalent to the original
statement. We can sum up these equivalences as follows:

Original Form	Means the Same as
1 Every *S* is *P*	1′ Every non*P* is non*S*
	1″ No *S* is non*P*
2 No *S* is *P*	2′ No *P* is *S*
	2″ Every *S* is non*P*
3 Some *S* is *P*	3′ Some *P* is *S*
4 Some *S* is not *P*	4′ Some non*P* is not non*S*
	4″ Every *S* is not *P*, or not every *S* is *P*

You may occasionally encounter, even outside of logic
books, some names for these equivalences: 2 and 2′ and
3 and 3′ are said to be *converse* to each other, and
changing from one to the other is called *conversion;*
1 and 1′ and 4 and 4′ are called *contrapositive* to each
other, and changing from one to the other is called
contraposition; 1 and 1″ and 2 and 2″ are called *ob-
verses* to each other, and changing from one to the
other is called *obversion.*

Finally, there are important relations between standard form statements that have the same subject and
the same predicate. If "Every Scot is thrifty" is true,
"Some Scot is not thrifty" must be false, and vice
versa. The same is true of "No Scot is thrifty" and
"Some Scot is thrifty." This relation is called *contradic-
tion* and these pairs of statements are said to be *con-*

tradictories. Contradictories cannot both be true *or* both be false; one must be true and the other false. But "Every Scot is thrifty" and "No Scot is thrifty" are *contraries;* they cannot both be true, but they can both be false (as in fact they are). "Some Scot is thrifty" and "Some Scot is not thrifty" cannot both be false, but they can both be true (as in fact they are). They are called *subcontraries.* If "Every Scot is thrifty" is true, then "Some Scot is thrifty" must be true too, but not vice versa, and the same relation holds between "No Scot is thrifty" and "Some Scot is not thrifty." The *Some* statements are the *subalterns* of the *Every* and *No* statements.

These relations cause no problems when we are talking about Scots, for there are such things as Scots, and some of them are thrifty and some are not. But a statement like "Every trespasser on my land will be shot" may be true even if there are no trespassers, and a statement like "No woman is a witch" is true because there are no witches. If we use subalternation on the first statement, we could derive "Some trespasser on my land will be shot." This statement could be converted to "Some person who will be shot is a trespasser on my land," which could be false even if the *Every* statement were true. Similarly, we could convert "No woman is a witch" to "No witch is a woman" and use subalternation to get "Some witch is not a woman." This statement sounds as if we are saying that there *are* male witches. Thus when we are talking about empty classes,[1] it is not safe to use subalternation.

It turns out that contraries and subcontraries also present problems. When we are talking, for example, about ghosts or unicorns, there are puzzling problems about just what statements are true and false. Are we to say that "Some ghost is fat" is true or false? What about "Some ghost is not fat," "Every ghost is fat," and "No ghost is fat"? There are no satisfactory answers, no answers, that is, acceptable to common sense and at the same time preserving these relations between standard form statements. Logicians are concerned

---

[1]An *empty class* is a class with no members, for example moons of Venus or horses on the moon.

with finding perfectly general rules which make no appeal outside of logic and sometimes leave contraries, subcontraries, and subalternates out of their systems because of these problems. But since these relations are sometimes useful for practical applications of logic, we will take a different course. We will continue to use these relations, but with a warning flag attached to them to remind us that these relations do not hold for statements about empty classes.

Two common mistakes should be mentioned here. First, it is easy to confuse contraries and contradictories. That every man is honest may be false, but is no proof that no man is honest, only that some men are not honest. Contraries *can* both be false, and often are. Second, if we find that some women are emotional, it may be that every woman is and it may be that some are and some are not. The truth of the subalternate neither proves nor disproves the truth of the statement of which it is the subalternate.

A handy way of representing these relations is the square of opposition, pictured below. Light lines mark the relations that hold only for statements about nonempty classes.

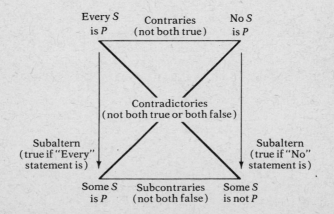

SYLLOGISMS

A *categorical syllogism* (hereafter called simply a syllogism) is an argument composed of three standard

form statements, of which two are the premises and
the other is the conclusion. There must be only three
terms in these statements, and each statement must
contain two of these terms. Here is a typical syllogism:

> Every admirer of Beethoven is a true music-lover.
> Schroeder is an admirer of Beethoven.
> ———
> Schroeder is a true music-lover.

The first two statements are the premises, the third
the conclusion. The three terms are "Schroeder," which
appears twice as a subject term, "admirer of Beethoven," which appears once as a subject term and once
as a predicate term, and "true music-lover," which appears twice as a predicate term. The term which appears in both premises, but not in the conclusion, in
this case "admirer of Beethoven," is called the *middle*
term. The term which is the subject of the conclusion,
in this case "Schroeder," is called the *minor* term. And
the term which is the predicate of the conclusion, in
this case "true music-lover," is called the *major* term.
The premise in which the minor term appears is called
the *minor premise*, and that in which the major term
appears, the *major premise*.

Any argument which looks like a syllogism but has
more than three terms, or in which each of the three is
not used twice, is not a real syllogism. (It may be something else, as we will see in the next section.) A common type of pseudosyllogism has one term which
seems the same in both uses, but is not. For example

> Every friend of Charley Brown who can play is on
> Charley's baseball team.
> Sally Brown is a friend of Charley Brown who can play.
> ———
> Sally Brown is on Charley's baseball team.

may be a pseudosyllogism if in the first premise *play*
means play baseball, and in the second premise, play
games suitable for small children. Pseudosyllogisms are
not valid arguments. They are sometimes said to commit the Fallacy of Four Terms.

There are only a few patterns of syllogism which

give a valid argument. Any syllogism which does not fit into one of these argument forms is not valid. We will examine each of these in turn.

We will first write the syllogistic patterns in short hand form using *S* for the minor term, *P* for the major term, and *M* for the middle term. As before, *N* stands for an individual name. As we examine each pattern in turn, we will present clear examples of the valid form and diagrams similar to those already used in Chapter 7. We will represent complete classes or groups as whole circles, parts of classes or groups as segments of circles, and individuals as dots. The statement "Every bird is a migratory creature" states a relation between the whole class of birds (*Every* bird . . .) and the class of migratory creatures. But since birds are only part of the class of migratory creatures, we will represent this class as a segment of a circle. Here is the diagram:

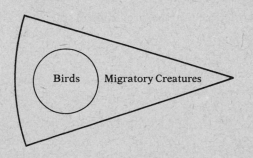

It represents the fact that the *whole* class of birds (complete circle) is contained within or makes up *part* of the class of migratory creatures (circle segment). If we diagram "No birds are mammals" we need two whole circles

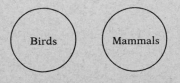

since the *whole* class of birds is outside of the *whole* class of mammals. No bird is part of the mammal class, no mammal is part of the bird class. "Some birds are pets" is diagrammed in this way

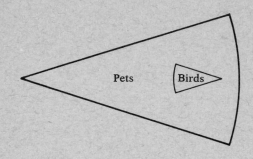

since *some* birds are part of the class of pets, and *some* pets are part of the class of birds. But "Some birds are not pets" must be diagrammed in this way

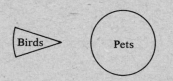

since what we want to say is that some birds are not any pet at all. Even if every bird were a pet, *some* birds (for example Cock Robin and Sam Sparrow) would not be *some pets* (for example Rocket and Augie Dog).

Think of a map: All of the state of Illinois is inside the United States. To show this we would show all of Illinois but only some of the United States. To show that some of Lake Superior is in Canada we need diagram only part of each. To show that no part of the Columbia River is in any part of Montana we must show all of both. To show that some of the Columbia River is outside any part of Washington state, we must show that section of the river and the whole territory of the state.

The diagrams for individuals and classes are even

simpler. "Woodstock is a bird" is diagrammed this way:

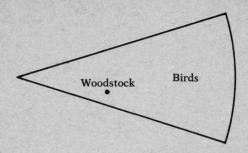

We diagram "Woodstock is not a mammal" this way:

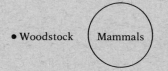

In the first case we have a circle segment, since Woodstock is in only one part of the class of birds; in the second we need a whole circle, since Woodstock is not in any part of the class of mammals.

Now let us examine the four valid patterns of syllogism. The first pattern starts with the premise:

$$\text{Every } M \text{ is } P$$

We then add the statement that an individual, or every member of a class S, or some members of a class S, are included in M, and get the conclusion that that individual, or every member of S, or some members of S (depending on which second premise we add) are included in class P. That is, we have three variations on this pattern:

Every M is P	Every M is P	Every M is P
N is M	Every S is M	Some S is M
N is P	Every S is P	Some S is P

To diagram these three variations we start as follows.

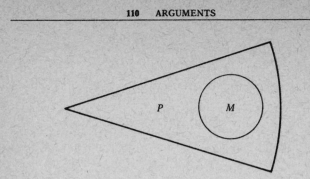

Then we add it to the appropriate premises:

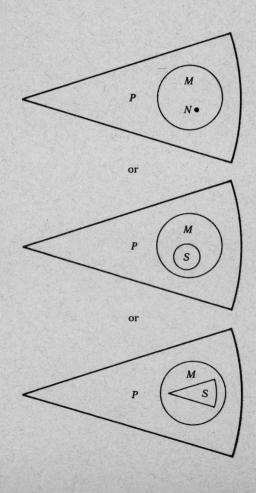

Looking at the diagrams we can see that if *N* is in *M* it *must* be in *P;* if all of class *S* is in *M*, all of class *S must* be in *P;* and if some of class *S* is in *M*, some of class *S must* be in *P*. Notice that we did not draw a *separate* diagram for "*N* is *M*," etc.; we used the *M* circle from the diagram of the first premises.

Examples of these variations on pattern 1 follow:

> Every bird is feathered.
> Woodstock is a bird.
> ———————————————
> Woodstock is feathered.

> Every bird is feathered.
> Every sparrow is a bird.
> ———————————————
> Every sparrow is feathered.

> Every bird is feathered.
> Some pet is a bird.
> ———————————————
> Some pet is feathered.

In the third variation, if the premise is "Some *M* is *S*" the pattern is not importantly different, since "Some *M* is *S*" is equivalent to "Some *S* is *M*." Thus

> Every bird is feathered.
> Some bird is a pet.
> ———————————————
> Some pet is feathered.

is a minor variation on the third version of our pattern. Since "Some *S* is *P*" is equivalent to "Some *P* is *S*," the conclusion of either variation could be "Some feathered creature is a pet" and we would still have essentially the same pattern.

The second pattern starts with the premise:

No *M* is *P*

To this we add the same three second premises as in the first pattern:

No *M* is *P*
N is *M*
_____
N is not *P*

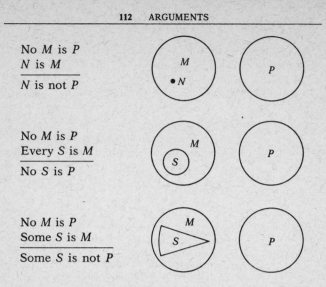

No *M* is *P*
Every *S* is *M*
_____
No *S* is *P*

No *M* is *P*
Some *S* is *M*
_____
Some *S* is not *P*

We can see that if *N* is inside *M* it must be outside *P;*
if all of *S* is in *M*, none of it can be inside *P;* and if
some of *S* is in *M*, some of it must be outside *P*. Examples of these variations are the following:

> No bird is four-legged.
> Woodstock is a bird.
> _____
> Woodstock is not four-legged.

> No bird is four-legged.
> Every sparrow is a bird.
> _____
> No sparrow is four-legged.

> No bird is four-legged.
> Some pet is a bird.
> _____
> Some pet is not four-legged.

As in pattern 1, we can get minor subvariations by converting any of the *some* statements. We can also get
subvariations by converting any of the *no* statements.
Again these variations make no difference: They would
not change the diagrams in any important way.

Pattern 3 starts with the premise:

Every *P* is *M*

The addition of either "No *S* is *M*" or "Some *S* is not *M*" gives us these syllogisms:

Every *P* is *M*
No *S* is *M*   or
────────────
No *S* is *P*

Every *P* is *M*
Some *S* is not *M*
────────────
Some *S* is not *P*

We can diagram these as:

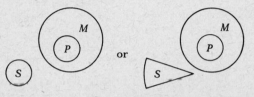

We have to show the complete *M* circle because of the nature of the second premise in each case; we must show that *S* is completely or partly outside of *M*, and to show this we need the whole *M* circle.

Examples of pattern 3 are as follows:

Every bird is hatched from an egg.
No pet of mine is hatched from an egg.
────────────
No pet of mine is a bird.

Every bird is hatched from an egg.
Some pet is not hatched from an egg.
────────────
Some pet is not a bird.

(Again, we can get minor variations by converting *no* or *some* statements.)

Finally, pattern 4 starts with the premise:

Every *M* is *S*

Adding the minor premise "Some *M* is *P*" or "Some *M* is not *P*" gives:

Every *M* is *S*
Some *M* is *P*
────────────
Some *S* is *P*

Every *M* is *S*
Some *M* is not *P*
────────────
Some *S* is not *P*

Both diagrams are a little puzzling. The first looks like the following.

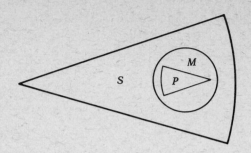

We can see that some *P* is *S*, which is equivalent to saying that some *S* is *P*.

The second diagram can most easily be drawn by labeling a circle segment as "non*P*," so the diagram looks like this:

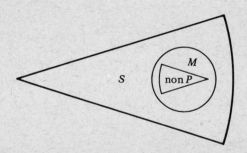

Since some non*P* is in *S*, some *S* is non*P*; that is to say, some *S* is not *P*.

Here are two examples:

> Every bird is feathered.
> Some bird is a pet.
> _____
> Some pet is feathered.

Every bird is feathered.
Some bird is not a pet.
_____
Some feathered creature is not a pet.

In all of these cases the examples are intuitively convincing, and the diagrams enable us to see why the conclusion follows from the premises. But some invalid arguments *sound* convincing and some invalid arguments *look* as if they fit the pattern. For example

Every *P* is *M*
Every *S* is *M*

Every *S* is *P*

can be made to sound convincing if we use the example

Every beagle has a tail.
Snoopy has a tail.

Snoopy is a beagle.

and diagram it as follows:

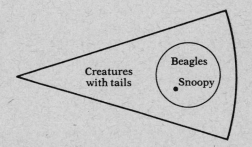

Now this particular argument has a true conclusion, but it has the pattern:

Every *P* is *M*

N is *M*

N is *P*

Here is another example of the pattern:

Every beagle has a tail.
Charley Brown's kite has a tail.

Charley Brown's kite is a beagle.

This argument is obviously a bad one. Even in the first argument the premises do not force us to diagram the conclusion in the way shown in any syllogism of this pattern. We can always diagram as follows:

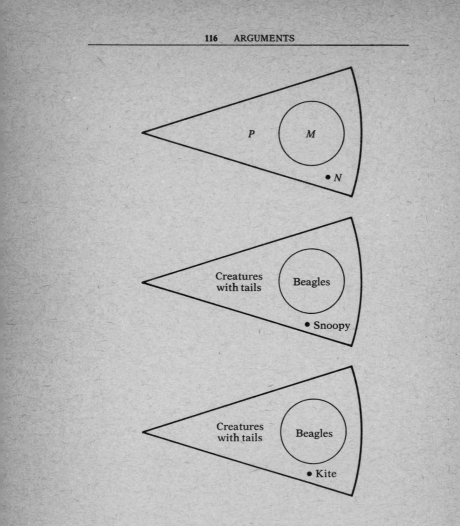

We see in pictorial form the difficulty with this syllogism; to have two things included in a third does not mean that they are included within each other. Incidentally, this is an instance of a fallacy known as *Excluded Middle*, which we might translate as "middle term out of a job" or "middle term not doing its job." Notice that in the valid argument which follows pattern 1, the middle term is literally in the middle, linking the major and minor terms. In the invalid argument the middle term fails to do this.

In the middle diagram we know Snoopy ought to go

in the *Beagles* circle not because of the argument but because of other information we possess. This pattern is untrustworthy because it *may* start with true premises and yet give us a false conclusion. In any of our four valid patterns, on the other hand, if the premises are true the conclusion *must* be true.

In any syllogism we suspect of being invalid we can use the techniques mentioned above. We can try to find an argument of the same pattern that has true premises and a false conclusion, *or* we can try to diagram the argument in such a way that both premises are correctly diagrammed but the conclusion is not diagrammed. Take, for example, this syllogism:

No beagle is really a World War I pilot.
Charley Brown is not really a World War I pilot.
_____
Charley Brown is not a beagle.

The conclusion is true, but is the pattern valid? The pattern is as follows:

$$No\ P\ is\ M$$
$$N\ is\ not\ M$$
$$\overline{N\ is\ not\ P}$$

Examine another example of this pattern:

No beagle is a cat.
Snoopy is not a cat.
_____
Snoopy is not a beagle.

The premises permit us to diagram as follows:

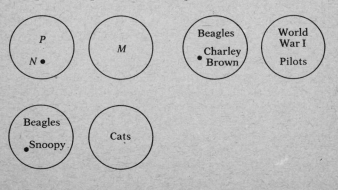

In the Charley Brown case the diagram is *in fact* mistaken; the *premises* do not rule out the diagram, our outside knowledge does. Thus we can see in two ways that syllogisms of this pattern are invalid. They may *accidentally* have true conclusions, but we cannot *count* on it even when they have true premises.

With these clues for recognizing invalid syllogisms and your knowledge of the four valid patterns (see the chart at the end of the chapter), you should be able to separate valid from invalid syllogisms in most cases.

It may also be helpful to remember a few rules of thumb. Every valid syllogism has one universal premise, which contains the middle term. No valid syllogism has two negative premises and no valid syllogism has two particular premises (*some* . . .). There are other rules for detecting invalid syllogisms, but some of them are rather complex.

It may seem troublesome to have to learn the four patterns and to practice applying them to actual arguments. In fact, however, this method of checking syllogisms is the simplest I can devise. Older methods of checking the validity of syllogisms by pattern require you to learn even more patterns, and modern methods of checking syllogisms by a set of rules requires you to remember five or six fairly complex rules and master some fairly complex distinctions. Since all of our patterns except the rarely encountered pattern are quite simple and easy to remember, the method described here is easier than any other I know of. There are 864 different ways of putting together syllogisms, and the valid forms and their variations constitute only about a dozen of these. So our work in learning to apply the four patterns may save us a great deal of trouble.

SORITESES AND ENTHYMEMES

Sometimes real-life arguments are expressed as neat, formal syllogisms. More often we reason in incomplete syllogisms, which are called *enthymemes,* and we sometimes encounter interlocking "chains" of syllogisms, which are called *soriteses.*

Consider, for example, an argument expressed in this way: "Sandy is a Scot, so of course he's thrifty."

If we add the implied premise, "Every Scot is thrifty,"
we get the pattern syllogism:

> Every Scot is thrifty.
> Sandy is a Scot.
> _____
> Sandy is thrifty.

Presumably the person who gave the first argument
intended us to understand the suppressed premise
"Every Scot is thrifty." Leaving premises unexpressed
in this way causes no trouble in many cases. But sometimes it may. If only *some* Scots are thrifty we get the
*in*valid pattern:

> Some Scot is thrifty.
> Sandy is a Scot.
> _____
> Sandy is thrifty.

Now, once we come to think about it, it is not really
very likely that every single Scot is thrifty. There must
be *some* extravagant Scots. Thus the argument is not
really a good one. If it is valid, one premise is not true;
and if we weaken that premise to be sure it is true then
the argument is invalid. In many arguments that have a
missing premise, the missing premise will not bear
close examination. Often we encounter arguments such
as "He's Jewish, so naturally . . . ," "He's black, so
naturally . . . ," "He's a cop, so naturally . . ." If we are
to regard these as syllogisms with missing premises,
then the missing premises are ones which cannot be
defended. The missing premise would have to be an
every (or in some cases a *no*) statement, and it is obvious in most cases that such sweeping generalities
cannot be established.

In other cases the missing premise may really be
too obvious to need stating. We can even use our patterns of valid syllogisms to figure out what the missing
premise must be if the argument is to be valid. If we
have two premises we can look at the valid patterns
and see what conclusion, if any, would follow. If we
have a conclusion and one premise, we can see whether
they match any of the patterns, and if so, what the

missing premise should be. For example, consider the argument:

No team with girls and dogs is going to get uniforms.
Every team managed by Charley Brown is a team with girls and dogs.

Even if the conclusion were not obvious, we could see that if this is going to be a valid argument it will fall into pattern 2. The conclusion must therefore be a *no* statement. "Team with girls and dogs" must be the middle term, since it appears in both premises. The conclusion, therefore, must state a relation between teams managed by Charley Brown and teams that are going to get uniforms. Since "No team managed by Charley Brown is going to get uniforms" means the same as "No team that is going to get uniforms is managed by Charley Brown," it does not really matter which we choose. Similarly, in the argument "Every believer in the Great Pumpkin is looking for a sincere pumpkin patch, so Linus is looking for a sincere pumpkin patch" we can see that the pattern must be the first one. "Believer in the Great Pumpkin" is the middle term, since it is not in the conclusion. To fit into pattern 1, the middle term must be the predicate of the missing premise, and the minor term, "Linus," the subject. So the missing premise is "Linus is a believer in the Great Pumpkin."

When we come to soriteses, interlocking chain syllogisms, we have a similar situation in some ways. The usual way of presenting a sorites is to give a set of premises, either giving the final conclusion or leaving it to be drawn. To reach the conclusion of the whole sorites we have to pair off two premises which have a common term and draw the conclusion which follows from them. Then we pair this conclusion off with another premise and draw a conclusion. We go on in this way until we have used all of the premises and reached a final conclusion, which is the conclusion of the whole sorites. Of course each syllogism must be of a valid pattern.

Here is an example adapted from Lewis Carroll, the author of *Alice in Wonderland:*

Everyone who really appreciates Beethoven keeps silent
         while the "Moonlight Sonata" is played.
Every guinea pig is hopelessly ignorant of music.
No one who is hopelessly ignorant of music keeps silent
         while the "Moonlight Sonata" is played.

To "solve" the sorites we pair off the first and third
premises, which have the common term "one who keeps
silent while the "Moonlight Sonata" is played," and
draw the conclusion "No one who really appreciates
Beethoven is hopelessly ignorant of music." We combine
this subconclusion with the second premise to draw
the conclusion of the whole sorites "No guinea pig
really appreciates Beethoven."

Soriteses like Carroll's are amusing puzzles, but we
rarely encounter them in real life. When we occasionally do, sometimes a premise is obviously left out, so
that we have a combination of enthymeme and sorites.
You will find a few examples of this sort in the problems at the end of this chapter. The ability to recognize
syllogisms, enthymemes, and soriteses and check their
validity is a skill worth acquiring, for despite the development of more powerful tools of logic, a great many
arguments which we encounter in books, newspapers,
and magazines, as well as on radio and television and
in conversation, can be judged in terms of these basically simple patterns.

To help you work the cases, a chart of the four valid
patterns of syllogisms and their variations is provided
on the following two pages. Beside each syllogism
form is the appropriate diagram. Here is how to use
the chart in checking a syllogism: 1. Replace the minor,
major, and middle terms by S, P, and M respectively.
2. See if there is a syllogism on the chart that has the
same pattern. Remember that the order of the premises,
conversion of No and Some premises, etc., can hide
similarities. 3. If there is no syllogism of the same
pattern on the chart, your syllogism is invalid. 4. If
there is a syllogism of the same pattern on the chart,
your syllogism is valid and you can identify the pattern
from the chart and draw the diagram.

Chart

Pattern 1

Every *M* is *P*
N is *M*
_____
N is *P*

Every *M* is *P*
Every *S* is *M*
_____
Every *S* is *P*

Every *M* is *P*
Some *S* is *M*
_____
Some *S* is *P*

Pattern 3

Every *P* is *M*
No *S* is *M*
_____
No *S* is *P*

Every *P* is *M*
Some *S* is not *M*
_____
Some *S* is not *P*

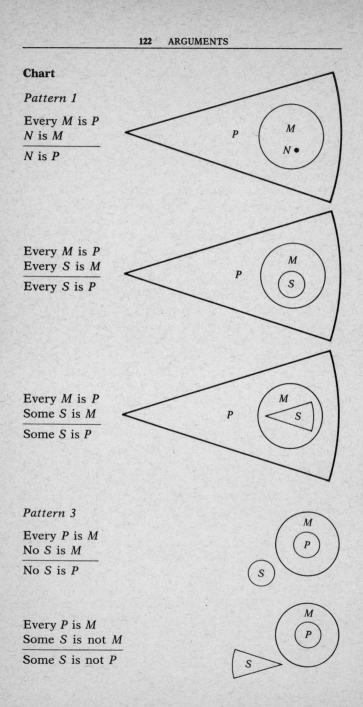

The Four Valid Patterns of Syllogisms

Pattern 2

No *M* is *P*
N is *M*
――――――
N is not *P*

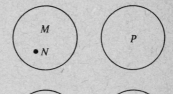

No *M* is *P*
Every *S* is *M*
――――――
No *S* is *P*

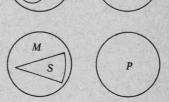

No *M* is *P*
Some *S* is *M*
――――――
Some *S* is not *P*

Pattern 4

Every *M* is *S*
Some *M* is *P*
――――――
Some *S* is *P*

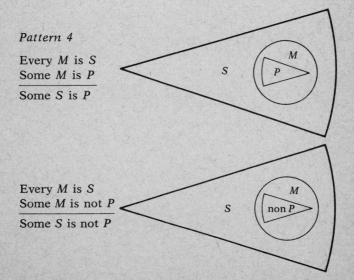

Every *M* is *S*
Some *M* is not *P*
――――――
Some *S* is not *P*

CASES

For each of the following statements give one statement which is true if the given statement is true, and one statement which is false if the given statement is true. It may help to put the given statement into strict standard form.

1. Every lion is fierce.
2. No lion drinks coffee.
3. Some pig is wild.
4. Some pig is not fat.
5. Gold is heavy.
6. No quadruped can whistle.
7. Nothing but gold will silence him.
8. Uneventful journeys are not worth writing about.
9. What is difficult needs attention.
10. Your visit is an unexpected pleasure.

Which of the following syllogisms are invalid? Give the pattern for each of the valid syllogisms. Draw a diagram for each of the syllogisms. (Note that the later examples are not in strict standard form.)

11. Every member of Charley Brown's team's under 3 feet tall.
Every one of Charley Brown's friends who lives in his neighborhood is on Charley Brown's team.

Every one of Charley Brown's friends who lives in his neighborhood is under 3 feet tall.

12. Every boy at camp with Charley Brown is interested in baseball.
Every friend of Charley Brown is interested in baseball

Every friend of Charley Brown is a boy at camp.

13. No boy or girl on Charley Brown's team is a good baseball player.
Every one of Charley Brown's friends in the neighborhood is a boy or girl on Charley Brown's team.

No one of Charley Brown's friends in the neighborhood is a good baseball player.

14. Every beagle respects the Head Beagle.
Snoopy is a Head Beagle.

Snoopy respects the Head Beagle.

15. No boy or girl on Charley Brown's team is a
good baseball player.
Snoopy is not a boy or girl on Charley Brown's team.

Snoopy is not a good baseball player.

16. Some of Charley Brown's friends are girls.
Every one of Charley Brown's friends likes baseball.

Some girls like baseball.

17. No beagle is really a World War I pilot.
Snoopy is a beagle.

Snoopy is not really a World War I pilot.

18. Every friend of Charley Brown is at camp in the
summer.
Some children are not at camp in the summer.

Some children are not friends of Charley Brown.

19. No friend of Charley Brown is a basketball player.
Some child in Charley Brown's neighborhood is a
basketball player.

Some child in Charley Brown's neighborhood is not
a friend of Charley Brown.

20. Every beagle is marked like Snoopy.
Not every beagle behaves like Snoopy.

Not every dog marked like Snoopy behaves like
Snoopy.

Find the missing premise or conclusion in each of the
following arguments. (It will help to put them in standard form.)

21. He is a fool, so he will soon be parted from his
money.
22. He is a good man, since he is kind to children.
23. She loves company because she is miserable.
24. She has saved a penny, so she has earned a penny.

25. Nobody knows the trouble I've seen, so nobody can understand me.
26. Every lion is fierce.
    Some lions do not drink coffee.
27. No fossil can be crossed in love.
    An oyster may be crossed in love.
28. No fool has become wealthy through his own efforts, but some millionaire has become wealthy through his own efforts. Only a fool would invest in that scheme of yours, so . . .
29. Students are never called for jury duty, but all eligible people are called sometime. So students must not be on the voting lists.
30. No shark ever doubts that it is well fitted out.
    A fish that cannot dance a minuet is contemptible.
    No fish is quite certain that it is well fitted out, unless it has three rows of teeth.
    All fishes except sharks are kind to children.
    No heavy fish can dance a minuet.
    A fish with three rows of teeth is not contemptible.
    Therefore . . .

CHAPTER 9
INDUCTION I

UNIVERSAL AND PARTICULAR

As we have already seen in our discussion of deductive logic, there is an important distinction between *Every* and *No* statements on the one hand and *Some* and *Some . . . not* statements on the other. *Every* and *No* statements, which are called *universal* statements, tell us something, either positive or negative, about every member of a group or class. *Some* and *Some . . . not* statements, which are called *particular* statements, give us information only about some members of a group or class. You may have noticed that statements about individuals behave in some ways more like universal statements than like particular ones. When we say "Snoopy is beagle" we are saying something about *every* Snoopy because we are talking only about one thing. Every individual can be regarded as a class with one member. (Of course Snoopy is in a class by himself in more ways than one!)

In this chapter we will consider a number of problems that arise from the relation between universal and particular. The part of logic that is called *Induction* is sometimes defined as reasoning from particular instances to universal generalizations, but this definition is not entirely satisfactory, as we shall see. It is only a pointer in the right direction. We can already see that the definition of deduction as reasoning from universal generalizations to particular instances is too narrow, since it includes only syllogistic reasoning—where every valid syllogism contains a universal statement—not propositional logic.

In connection with universal and particular there is often a misunderstanding of the way in which properties of groups or classes are related to properties of their subgroups or subclasses and of individuals in those groups or classes. We know from deductive logic that if *every* member of a class has a certain property, then any subclass, composed of some members of that class, and any individual member will have that property. If every beagle is four-footed, then American beagles are four-footed, and Snoopy is four-footed.

But a class as a whole can have certain properties that its members do not, and members of a class can individually have properties which the class as a whole lacks. For example people in other countries sometimes reason from "America is a very wealthy country" that each individual American is wealthy. The fallacy is partly one of ambiguity; *rich* does not mean quite the same in *rich country* as in *rich person*. Another fallacy involved is that of supposing a characterization of a group as a whole can be applied in a simple fashion to each individual in that group. To take a similar example "Russia is a Communist country" means that its government is Communist; Communism is the official philosophy taught in the schools; it affects the books that are published, the news that is reported; and so on. But this does not mean that each individual Russian is a Communist. Some reject some parts of Communist theory, such as its official atheism, others are opposed to Communism as a whole, secretly or even openly.

Another fallacy of the same kind is that of expecting the characteristics of each individual in a group to apply in a simple way to the group as a whole. An obvious example is that of a group of a hundred people, each weighing under 200 pounds. The group as a whole, of course, weighs far over 200 pounds. There are less obvious cases: A group of intelligent people does not always act intelligently, a group of civilized people does not always act in a civilized way.

This point is worth emphasizing because of our natural tendency to be lazy in thinking about groups and individuals. We hold a certain stereotyped idea of a group and expect all of its members to conform to that stereotype, or we judge all members of a group by the actions of a few whom we happen to have encountered.

Being clear about the exact meaning of general statements can be helpful. For example "Americans are the world's wealthiest people" means that the *average* American income is higher than the *average* income in other countries. Nevertheless the world's richest man might be a Greek or an Englishman, the world's poorest man might be an American. Many individual Americans are poorer than individual Europeans or Asians, or even than the average European or Asian. "Americans are the world's wealthiest people" does *not* mean that every American is wealthier than any person from another country.

If Americans are, on the average, wealthier than other people, we might expect that, other things being equal, there is a good chance that a given American would be wealthier than a given European or Asian or African. But we need to be cautious here. What do we mean by *other things being equal,* and *a good chance?* One thing that we might mean is that an American selected at random is likely to be wealthier than a person from another nation selected at random. By *selected at random* we mean that each person in each of the groups we are choosing from has an equal chance of being selected. By way of example, consider people listed in the New York telephone directory and people listed in the Paris telephone directory. If New Yorkers with listed phones are wealthier on the average than Parisians with listed phones, we would expect that if we selected people at random from the New York directory and paired them with people selected at random from the Paris directory, then in *most* cases (not all) the New Yorker would be the richer of the two.

Another thing we might expect, if Americans are wealthier than others, is that given groups of Americans would be wealthier on the whole than corresponding groups from other countries. There might be some groups or occupations in other countries that are wealthier than similar groups in America, but in the majority of such pairings we would expect to find the Americans richer. Thus American doctors would be wealthier than, say, English doctors, American plumbers wealthier than, for example, Italian plumbers, and so on. Again, a given English doctor might be richer than a given American doctor, but one randomly selected from a list of American Medical Association members would in most cases be richer than one randomly selected from the British Medical Association.

Since generalizations are often put vaguely or loosely, it is useful to ask ourselves just what is being asserted. If someone says "Americans are . . . ," "Negroes are . . . ," "Jews are . . . ," does he mean that *every* member of the group he is talking about has that characteristic? Does he mean that *on the average* the group has that characteristic (with the sort of consequences we have just been considering)? Or does he mean something else? Whichever he means, what sort of evidence does he have to back up this generalization? (Is he, for example, generalizing after having observed only a few members of the group?)

GENERALIZATION

People sometimes talk as if any generalization is suspect, and that the solution to the problems considered in the last section is to avoid generalization altogether. But this solution would be worse than the problems. Generalization, like classification, is an essential tool for dealing with the world; most of our useful knowledge about the world consists of generalizations. The solution is not to avoid making them, but rather to learn how to make *sound* generalizations firmly based on the best evidence available.

We can begin by considering a fairly trivial case, generalization based on observation of every member of a class. It is safe enough to generalize that all my children are boys when I have only two children, both boys. Such a *descriptive generalization*, as we shall call it, rarely gives us information of much value. It is not useful for prediction. I might have more children and one might be a girl. The important kind of generalization is *inductive;* it is made on the basis of observing only some members of a class in question. Some inductive generalizations are *universal*, attributing a characteristic to every member or no member of a class. But many are *statistical generalizations*, attributing a characteristic to a stated percentage of the members of a class.

Obviously, in many cases we must be content with inductive generalizations. Consider a manufacturer of flashbulbs. If too high a percentage of his flashbulbs misfire, he will lose business. So he wants to know the percentage of failures in the bulbs he is currently turning out. He could fire every flashbulb and make a descriptive generalization. But he would then have no product to sell. Instead he insures quality control by firing *some* of the flashbulbs and figuring out from the results what proportion of his total production is likely to misfire.

Such problems are handled by *statistical inference*, which involves applying certain mathematical principles to situations in the real world. The details of statistical inference are complex and belong to the science of statistics, and anyone who faces such problems frequently would be wise to take a course in statistics or hire a good statistician. But there are certain general principles of statistical reasoning that can be discussed in nonmathematical terms. They can help us deal with everyday problems of making inductive generalizations.

In giving these principles we will adopt the statistician's terms *sample* and *population*. By a *population* we mean the whole class—about which we are making a generalization—or the total number of observations—which would enable us to make a descriptive generalization. By a *sample* we mean those members of the class actually observed, or the observations actually made. When we reason inductively we reason from sample to population. For example suppose that we are trying to find out how each American will vote in the next Presidential election. Suppose also that we are interested simply in votes for or against a certain candidate. Our population in this case would be a total set of answers to the question "Will you vote for or against Candidate X?" by everyone who plans to vote. Our sample would be the set of answers we actually obtain by asking some voters how they plan to vote. More loosely we could refer to our sample as *voters questioned* and our population as *all voters*. Statisticians prefer to think of samples and populations as sets of observations or data; nonstatisticians usually think of them as sets of persons or things. The statistician's way of thinking about samples and populations is actually better, since we are interested only in some aspect of the group of people or things. But even statisticians sometimes fall into the looser popular way of talking, and where no confusion is likely to arise I will not always be fussy about this point.

We can now consider a few general rules for making generalizations:

1. Other things being equal, the larger the sample you use the better.

Other things, however, are not always equal. The flash-bulb manufacturer can fire only a certain number of tests without destroying his profits. An election survey must generally be done within a limited budget. Moreover, when the other rules we will give are satisfied, we can often get a surprisingly large amount of information from a surprisingly small sample. Under fairly ideal conditions a small sample can give sufficient information. It can happen that the amount of time or effort involved in making a sample larger will not yield enough additional information to be worthwhile.

2. Use your whole sample, do not pick and choose.

If you ignore any part of the information available for any reason, you are likely to destroy the validity of your results. Almost any conclusion can be made plausible by collecting a large amount of data and then discarding all the data that does not fit the desired conclusion. Even in an honest attempt to gather data we may be tempted to discard certain data as untypical or as observational error when these very data may actually be an indication that our conclusions must be modified or discarded. Some data may be discounted in the long run, but none should simply be "swept under the rug."

3. Select your sample in such a way that every member of the class in question has an equal chance of being selected.

Most people have a very crude idea of what constitutes a random sample. A sidewalk survey on a downtown street may discriminate against mothers kept at home by young children, minority groups who tend to shop in their own neighborhoods, and so on. Telephone surveys are biased against those who are too poor to own phones. At a time when economic issues were crucial, the Roosevelt-Landon election poll conducted by the now-defunct magazine *Literary Digest* failed badly for that reason. The *Literary Digest* used addresses from phone books in mailing a written survey. Those who could afford phones in the depressed economic situation of the early 1930s were much more likely to vote for the Republican, Landon, than was the general public. Sociologists now argue that written surveys of any kind are biased against those who lack middle-class habits of dealing with written material, and that personal surveys can be affected by interviewers' tendencies to avoid people who do not look respectable.

4. If there are within the class being sampled subclasses that might have variations with respect to the characteristic in question, choose samples from each such subclass in proportion to its percentage of the whole class.

You will notice that good surveys often break down results by significant groups (for example, men, women, under 30, over 30 on women's rights; regional and racial groups on civil rights; etc.). But it is equally important to take the different groups *and their percentage of the whole population* into account in reaching an overall conclusion. In complex cases, statistical expertise is needed to do so. However, major disproportions are fairly easy to see. For example, popularity or unpopularity of an issue or person on college campuses must be weighed against the fact that college students are less than 5 percent of the total population.

Disproof of generalizations is simple in the case of universal generalizations, complex in the case of statistical generalizations. If I claim that every Scot is thrifty, one extravagant Scot will disprove my generalization. If I am content to claim that 90 percent of Scots are thrifty, a disproof is much harder. Roughly speaking, a statistical generalization becomes more and more doubtful if samples taken from the class in question (observing all the cautions in rules 1–4) are not what you would expect if the generalization were true. We will say more about this point in the next chapter, when we discuss more complex forms of inductive inference.

CAUSE AND EFFECT

One important kind of generalization states a causal relation between two kinds of events, for example "Cigarette smoking causes lung cancer." Such generalizations are more complex than the kind of generalizations that we have been considering, but they fall into the same general categories. They can be descriptive, as in "Every major European war in this century has been caused by German aggression." They can be universal, as in "Every case of lung cancer is caused by smoking" or "Every case of smoking causes lung cancer." Neither of these, however, is what we normally mean by "Smoking causes lung cancer." Rather, we mean to say that smoking a certain amount for a certain period of time significantly increases the probability of lung cancer; this is a statistical generalization.

An important distinction with regard to causes is

the distinction between *necessary conditions* (sometimes called *necessary causes*), *sufficient conditions* (or *causes*), and *necessary and sufficient conditions* (or *causes*). *A* is a necessary condition of *B* if without *A*, *B* cannot occur. Thus the presence of oxygen is a necessary condition for combustion. *A* is a sufficient condition for *B* if the occurrence of *A* always causes the occurrence of *B*. Thus having your head cut off and being drowned are *both* sufficient conditions for death; of course so are many other events. *A* is the necessary and sufficient condition of *B* if *A* causes *B* and *nothing but A* causes *B*. So far as we now know, the attainment of critical mass is a necessary and sufficient condition for an atomic explosion.

When we talk of *the* cause of an event, we very often mean none of these but rather some event that combines with factors already present to make up a sufficient cause. Thus we say that the cause of a certain forest fire was a campfire which was not doused. But since undoused campfires do not always cause forest fires, it was not by itself the sufficient condition. Other factors such as dry weather, presence of combustible material near the campfire, etc., had to combine with the undoused fire to cause the conflagration.

Notice the reasoning we use here; *A* is not the sufficient condition of *B* if *A* can occur without *B* occurring. This follows from the definition of *sufficient condition*. Similarly, if *B* can occur even if *A* has not occurred, then *A* cannot be a *necessary* condition of *B*. And if *either B* occurs when *A* does not *or B* does not occur when *A* does, then *A* cannot be the necessary and sufficient condition of *B*.

We cannot reverse this reasoning. *A* can always be followed by *B* without being a sufficient condition of *B*. Night always follows day, but day does not *cause* night. *A* can always be present when *B* occurs without being a necessary condition of *B*. It is probably true that every person who has written a logic book has had toes, but having toes is not a necessary condition for writing a logic book. Even if *A* and *B* are always found together it does not show that *A* is the necessary and

sufficient cause of *B*. Every animal with a backbone
has lungs, and every animal with lungs has a backbone,
but neither state of affairs causes the other.

However, the fact that *A* always comes before *B* is
some evidence that *A* is a sufficient condition of *B*. The
fact that *B* never occurs when *A* is absent is some evidence that *A* is a necessary condition of *B*. And the
fact that *A* and *B* are always found together is some
evidence that one is the necessary and sufficient condition of the other.

What more do we need than this? Consider the relation between writing logic books and having toes. We
are sure that having toes is not a necessary condition
for writing logic books because we know of no reason
why lacking toes should prevent anyone from writing
a logic book. In other words we have no reason to
suppose that "No person without toes can write a
logic book" is a true generalization. On the other hand,
we believe that the presence of oxygen *is* a necessary
condition for combustion because we do have reason
to suppose that the generalization "No combustion can
take place without oxygen" is a true one. Thus our
reasons for accepting or rejecting causal generalizations are tied to our expectations about what is or is
not possible in the world as we know it. Our reasons
for regarding certain states of affairs as possible (for
example toeless logicians) and others as not possible
(for example combustion without oxygen) are connected with our ideas about the universe, which are
based on the findings of science. In the next chapter
we will consider certain questions about the methods
of science and their relation to statistical reasoning
and common sense.

CASES

Criticize the following arguments:

1. America is a capitalist country. Abbie is an American, so Abbie is a capitalist.

2. Timothy and his friends, who are Americans, use
LSD, so Americans must approve of the use of LSD.

3. Americans speak English. Little Concha Garcia is

an American citizen, so of course she speaks English.

4. America is a more powerful country than Greece, so American generals are more powerful than Greek generals.

5. America is ahead of Russia in space exploration, so the average American is more interested in space exploration than the average Russian.

What is likely to be wrong with the evidence for the following generalizations?

6. Of the experimental animals treated with the new serum, 50 percent showed signs of improvement. Unfortunately, the other guinea pig ran away, and we do not know what happened to it.

7. Women reject the goals of Women's Liberation. In a recent survey, three groups of women selected at random rejected the Women's Liberation Front demands for equal pay for equal work, free day care for children, and abortion on demand. The exact figures follow:

	Percent		
	For	Against	Undecided
St. Mary's Convent	0	100	0
Bethany Home for Retired Gentlewomen	11	72	17
Downtown YWCA	32	62	6

8. Mexican-American citizens reject *Chicano Power*. In a recent survey, Mexican-American citizens in our community rejected the demands of extremist Chicano Power groups. A questionnaire was mailed to all householders in the city with Spanish-American names. Of the 2517 questionnaires mailed, 890 were returned. Of these, 120 were not properly filled out. Of the remaining 770, 430 rejected the demands of the group, 206 approved of them, and 134 expressed mixed opinions.

9. "I have never met a woman who approves of the demands of the Women's Liberation movement," de-

clares Bishop Charles O'Toole, "except a few poor demented creatures who picketed my residence last week, and I do not count them. I am sure that all normal women reject these demands."

10. "American parents are not opposed to school busing programs," declares the superintendent of schools in Berkeley, California. "We have had such a program in Berkeley for a number of years, and it has worked out quite satisfactorily."

What would be adequate evidence both for and against each of the following causal generalizations?

11. Use of marijuana is a necessary condition for heroin addiction.

12. Use of marijuana is a sufficient cause for heroin addiction.

13. The contraceptive pill is the cause of the increase in sexual permissiveness.

14. The decline of religious belief is the cause of the increase in sexual permissiveness.

15. The rise of scientific thought is a sufficient cause for the decline of religious belief.

CHAPTER 10
INDUCTION II

SCIENTIFIC METHOD

In our discussion of abduction in Chapter 6 we saw that the method of hypothesis has something in common with the methods of science. But it is not until we begin to *test* our hypotheses that we begin to approach the real method of science. As C. S. Lewis points out in discussing the history of science:

> *Mere empiricists like Telesius or Bacon achieved nothing. What was fruitful in the thought of the scientists was the bold use of mathematics in the construction of hypotheses, tested not by observation simply but by controlled observation of phenomena that could be precisely measured. On the practical side it was this that delivered Nature into our hands.*[1]

Lewis correctly points out certain things which are characteristic of modern science: 1. Hypotheses are stated clearly and precisely, often in mathematical terms. 2. Hypotheses are tested by controlled observation. 3. Tests involve precise measurement.

Consider, for example, the explanation of certain phe-

[1]*English Literature in the Sixteenth Century*, Oxford University Press, New York, 1954, p. 3.

nomena involving vacuums near the beginnings of modern science. The older explanation of these phenomena was that "nature hates a vacuum," and that when a vacuum is created nature tries to fill it immediately. However, this explanation did not account for the fact that a vacuum pump would only raise a column of water to a certain height, and would raise heavier materials, such as mercury, to a lesser height.

Torricelli and Galileo explained these phenomena by postulating a "sea of air" that exerts pressure. When the vacuum pump creates a vacuum, air pressure forces the liquid into the gap. But since the pressure exerted by the air is finite, it can raise a column of liquid of only a certain height and weight. Furthermore, the pressure can be calculated, roughly at first then more precisely. Predictions based on the known pressure and the weight of the liquid to be raised can be made precisely and verified by controlled experiments. The older hypothesis, on the other hand, is vague and does not permit precise, controlled tests.

This method, which has characterized science at least since the time of Galileo, is usually called the *hypothetico-deductive method. Hypothetico* because it involves putting forth a hypothesis, *deductive* because consequences are deduced from this hypothesis and then tested. It is important to remember that the hypothesis must be clear if it is to be testable; the consequences that are to be deduced from it must also be precise. They must also be of a kind which *can* be tested by observation or experiment.

All of this is important to the nonscientist for several reasons. First, in our society science is greatly respected. All kinds of attempts are made to borrow the prestige of science for other enterprises—commercial, political, even religious. If we know something about the actual methods of science we are in a better position to judge such attempts.

Second, we can often borrow the techniques of science to deal with problems that confront us in everyday life. In our thinking about a wide variety of problems, whether the problem is gas mileage or the results of a social policy, we can attempt to form clear hypotheses, deduce precise consequences from them, and test these by controlled observation. It must be emphasized that the *source* of the hypotheses is of no relevance so far as scientific method is concerned. The source of scientific creativity is a matter for psychology and perhaps for philosophy. From the logician's point of view, so long as the hypothesis is clear and has testable consequences, whether it originates in a dream, a hunch, or thoughtful speculation does not weigh against it. Of course, as a matter of practical policy we may not want to waste our time checking out every bright idea or wild hunch. But in theory no hypothesis with testable consequences is disproved until one of those consequences is observed to be false. Of course, *not disproved* does not mean proved, nor even worth taking seriously.

Some hypotheses are so vague that no consequences can be drawn from them. Where this fault is due merely to hastiness or carelessness, we can sometimes make them more precise by asking the person who puts forward the hypothesis what he really means. In other cases, what would falsify or confirm a given hypothesis is so unclear that we are inclined to dismiss the hypothesis as meaningless. We reason that if a person knows what he means, he should know what will prove or disprove his meaning; if he does not know what will prove or disprove it, he does not really know what he means.

Some philosophers have taken this seemingly common-sense position and erected it into a philosophical principle. Taking *testable consequences* in a fairly narrow sense, they characterized ethical and religious statements as meaningless on the grounds that they have no testable consequences. This philosophical position is called *Logical Positivism*, and the Positivist version of the *if meaningful then provable or disprovable* principle is called the *verification principle.* Contemporary philosophers have largely rejected the Logical Positivist position, although its influence may still be found in the writings of some present-day scientists.

One major difficulty with the Positivist position is that the verification principle proved impossible to state so that it would rule out as meaningless whatever the Positivists wanted to exclude—religious and ethical statements—but not rule out certain scientific statements that the Positivists wished to retain. The fatal difficulty, however, is that the verification principle itself cannot be proved (or disproved for that matter) by the methods that the principle itself lays down. These methods are, roughly speaking, the methods of mathematics and empirical science. But the verification principle is a philosophical principle, unprovable by mathematical or scientific means. Thus the principle is self-refuting.

Of course the principle could be said not to apply to itself, to be an exception to its own rule. But if there were to be one such exception, why could there not be others? Various attempts were made to save the verification principle by giving it some special status, as for an example a recommendation about how language should be used, an analysis of what is meant by *true* or *provable*, a presupposition of scientific method, and so on. But this left open the possibility of making several different recommendations about language, several different analyses of what is meant by *true* or *provable*, several different suggestions as to what is presupposed by scientific method. There must be some reason or basis in argument for choosing one of these recommendations or analyses or suggestions rather than another. But the method of decision between the alternatives could not be the verification principle itself: That would be begging the question. So at least one kind of important question would have to be settled by some other method. If that is true, then it might equally well be the case that ethical questions, or questions of literary criticism, or theological questions might have their own appropriate methods and tests. Even the attempt to save the verification principle left the door open to philosophy, and therefore for ethical and perhaps for religious statements and arguments.

A moral to be drawn from this discussion is that ambiguity may exist in the application of the term *scientific method*. It may mean the hypothetico-deductive method with its insistence on clear hypotheses and testable consequences. But an appeal to scientific method may also conceal lingering traces of the Positivist position—the demand that statements in areas outside of science or mathematics be subject to the same procedures of proof and disproof as statements in science or mathematics. Most philosophers nowadays would agree that the attempt to apply scientific method in this Positivistic sense to religion, ethics, literary criticism, law, politics, history, etc., is a mistake. History, for example, obviously has its own standards of proof and disproof that rest on documents (in a wide sense) and their interpretation. Theology, literary criticism, etc., by the same argument have their own standards and their own methods. That these are different from the methods of science or mathematics does not mean that they are inferior.

STATISTICAL METHODS

In the last chapter we discussed briefly some principles of statistical reasoning. Since these methods are becoming increasingly important in such sciences as psychology, sociology, and education, which are likely to affect us directly, it would be wise to take a little closer look at statistical reasoning.

Descriptive statistics has to do with presenting information in tables, charts, graphs, etc., in such a way that the information can be grasped easily and an accurate idea formed of the relation of factors. This form of statistics is the most familiar to the layman, since he often sees descriptive statistics in newspapers and magazines, on television, and so on.

More important, however, and more closely related to scientific method is *statistical inference*. In statistical inference we decide among hypotheses—about a population, for example—on the basis of observations of samples from that population. Frequently we are faced with a case where only two hypotheses need be considered, for example that a given treatment does or does not cure a certain disease, that smoking does *or* does not increase the chances of getting lung cancer, etc. In such cases statisticians often speak of a *null hypothesis* and an *alternative hypothesis*. The null hypothesis is usually the *no change, no difference*, or *no significance* hypothesis, for example that the treatment has no effect on the disease or that smoking does not increase the chances of getting lung cancer. The alternative hypothesis is usually the *change, difference*, or *significance* hypothesis; for example that the treatment does help to cure the disease, that smoking does increase the chance of lung cancer. In many cases the consequences of the null hypothesis can be found by looking at either what has happened in the past or what happens when the situation is not interfered with, or else by calculating what will happen by chance. Thus in the treatment-disease case the consequence of the null hypothesis would be that patients given the new treatment will have the same rate of recovery as patients have had in the past or as patients who are not given the treatment. In the cigarette-cancer case, the consequence of the null hypothesis would be that smokers will have the same proportion of lung cancer as nonsmokers.

That the observed consequences do not agree with the consequences of the null hypothesis may or may not be significant. Random variations do occur in different groups, and factors other than those being investigated may be at work. Thus we must be sure that any departures from the consequences predicted by the null hypothesis are not due to chance or to some unsuspected factor. For example patients given a new treatment may do better than patients not given that treatment as the accidental result of increased attention by the nurses. A selected group of smokers may by chance be more prone to lung cancer than the selected group of nonsmokers. In order to judge such possibilities we need to be sure we are aware of all the relevant factors in the situation, and we also need to know something about the probabilities involved.

Where these are complex we may need actuarial records of the kind kept by insurance companies or expertise in calculating probabilities. In some cases, however, such calculations are relatively easy. Consider

a simple experiment in behavioristic psychology. A rat
is sent through a T-shaped maze and turns either left
or right at the top of the T. He is then sent through
the maze again. Is he more likely to choose the same
turn he made before, the opposite turn, or is it a
matter of chance which turn he will make? The null
hypothesis here is that the first turn will have no
effect on the second turn, and thus that the turn
sequences right-right, right-left, left-right, and left-left
are equally likely and will in the long run occur with
approximately equal frequency (just as in tossing a
coin twice, where the sequences head-head, head-tail,
tail-head, and tail-tail each have equal probability and
will occur equally frequently in the long run). Experimental evidence proves the null hypothesis false. Rats
choose the previously unexplored arm of the T maze
in a significantly large number of cases: The sequences
right-left and left-right occur far more frequently than
we would expect on the basis of chance, and the sequences right-right and left-left occur far less frequently. This is technically known as *alternation behavior*. There is an interesting body of work in psychology that deals with it. Our purpose in mentioning
it, however, is merely to illustrate the relatively simple
probability calculations involved in drawing the consequences of the null hypothesis.

In some cases, we need to have certain information
about the population before we can make meaningful
tests of our hypotheses about it. There are some statistical methods, called *nonparametric* methods that
need relatively little information of this kind.

An ingenious and easily understandable example of
nonparametric methods is the *sign test*. Consider the
null hypothesis that there is no significant difference
in IQ between two groups. Some methods of testing
would involve knowing the average IQ in each group,
the extent of variation from the average in each group,
and other similar factors. In using the sign test we
simply make random pairings of persons from each
group and subtract the IQ of the persons in the second group from the IQ of the persons in the first group.
If the IQ of the members of the second group is

larger, we of course get a minus number. We count the·plus and minus numbers. If there is actually no significant difference in IQ, we would expect the numbers of pluses and minuses to be approximately equal. If the difference in the number of pluses and minuses is significantly different we can reject the null hypothesis and accept the alternative hypotheses, that there is a difference in intelligence between the groups.

In any statistical inference there are two dangers. One is the danger of rejecting a true hypothesis and the other of accepting a false one. These dangers are to some extent complementary. By minimizing one risk we frequently increase the other. An extremely suspicious person, for example, may accept few false hypotheses but in doing so undoubtedly rejects many true ones. Ideally, we should avoid both risks insofar as possible.

In this very brief and necessarily incomplete survey of statistical reasoning, we have concentrated on nontechnical matter that is likely to be of practical use in everyday reasoning. A good book on statistics[2] or the services of a competent statistician are useful for more advanced work.

SCIENCE AND SENSE

In view of the widespread respect for science in our society, it may be well to mention some areas where a healthy skepticism about science may be necessary. We would do well to take scientific claims with a grain of salt in these circumstances:

1. When the findings of science genuinely contradict your own experience.

Apparent conflicts, of course, are to be expected. The earth *looks* flat. The sun *appears* to be moving, and so on. Science explains these apparent facts and sets them in a wider framework. We learn why things appear as they do, or why they are not really as they

[2]Two excellent books are: W. A. Wallis and H. V. Roberts, *Statistics, A New Approach*, Free Press, New York, 1956. P. A. Games and G. R. Klare, *Elementary Statistics*, McGraw-Hill, New York, 1967.

appear. But sometimes there are actual conflicts. Some of the early behaviorists, for example, denied that human beings were really conscious. Now either this was a misuse of language—they meant something different by consciousness than is ordinarily meant—or they were contradicting the experience of every human being (including themselves). No matter what their reasoning, there must have been a flaw in it. And indeed there was—more than one! As another example, until the recent research by Masters and Johnson, many sexologists denied the existence of multiple orgasms within a short period of time in women, contradicting the personal experience of some women. Perhaps few of us are so respectful of science as to trust it when it directly contradicts our own experience. But there is some tendency in our society to trust the results of "the latest research" rather than the experience of individuals, even where the research is highly questionable and the individuals extremely worthy of credit. This is especially noticeable in the area of education, but is making itself felt in other areas.

2. When science wanders
into areas beyond its competence.

Science, simply *as* science, has nothing in particular to say about moral or artistic values, or about metaphysical or religious questions. To take an example of the illegitimate extension of science into these areas, consider the theory of evolution. The evolution of living things by a process of variation, competition, and survival of the fittest—the process called *natural selection*—is a well-established scientific theory. The theory has nothing in particular to say about the origin of the process of natural selection or any ultimate goal of the process. Most variations are unfavorable to survival; the organisms which survive are *fittest* only in the sense of surviving in a certain set of conditions. If the conditions change, that adaptation may become unfavorable to survival.

Some scientists and admirers of science have taken this well-established, relatively modest theory and applied it to areas where it has no real application. They speak of the "evolution" of the universe, whereas the theory is well-established only for the evolution of living species. They speak as if evolution were necessarily a process of improvement, whereas there is no basis for this in the well-established theory. They try to derive ethical systems from the facts of evolution. Both the philosophy of ruthless competition and the philosophies of self-development and cooperation have been justified as evolutionary. But the well-established theory is descriptive, and says nothing about values.

In fact, popular evolutionism is an example of a familiar process of illegitimately extending into areas beyond its competence whatever intellectual discipline is at the moment successful and prestigious. It happened to mathematics in the seventeenth century, and we had "mathematical" ethics, metaphysics treated like Euclidian geometry, and so on. A similar process has been going on in the nineteenth and twentieth centuries. Communism, for example, still claims to be a scientific philosophy of man, although the failure of predictions drawn from its theories would be sufficient to cause rejection many times over of a genuinely scientific theory.

3. Where science contradicts your own expertise or your own carefully checked reasoning.

I find a good, if somewhat controversial, example in C. S. Lewis's critique of the science of biblical criticism. Lewis's first criticism of modern biblical criticism is based on his own expertise as a scholar of literature:

> Whatever these men may be as Biblical critics, I distrust them as critics. They seem to me to lack literary judgment, to be imperceptive about the very quality of the texts they are reading. . . . If [a man] tells me that something in a Gospel is a legend or romance, I want to know how many legends and romances he has read, how well his palate is trained in detecting them by the flavor.[3]

[3]"Modern Theology and Biblical Criticism," in *Christian Reflections*, Wm. B. Eerdmans, Grand Rapids, Michigan, 1967, p. 154.

Lewis's second criticism has to do with the claim that "the real behavior and purpose and teaching of Christ came very rapidly to be misunderstood by His followers and has been recovered or exhumed only by modern scholars."[4] Lewis cites as evidence the failure of similar claims in other cases, for example in the case of Plato. His third criticism is of "a constant use of the principle that miracles do not occur."[5] Lewis's own reasoning[6] leads him to challenge this claim.

Finally, Lewis criticizes the reconstructions of the origins of New Testament documents. Here he speaks not only as a literary expert but as an author who has found the origins of his own works and those of his friends completely misconstrued by contemporary reviewers. Lewis argues as follows:

> Consider with what overwhelming advantage the [contemporary] reviewers start. They reconstruct the history of a book written by someone whose mother-tongue is the same as theirs; a contemporary, educated like themselves, living in something like the same mental and spiritual climate. They have everything to help them. The superiority in judgment and diligence which you are going to attribute to the Biblical critics will have to be almost superhuman if it is to offset the fact that they are everywhere faced with customs, language, race-characteristics, class-characteristics, and basic assumptions which no scholarship will ever enable any man now alive to know as surely and intimately and instinctively as the reviewer can know mine.[7]

And yet, says Lewis, the reconstructions of the contemporary critics have in his experience been 100 percent false!

Now this particular example may be ill chosen, for it

[4]*Christian Reflections*, p. 157.
[5]*Christian Reflections*, p. 158.
[6]For example, in his book *Miracles*, Macmillan, New York, 1947.
[7]*Christian Reflections*, p. 161.

may engage your sympathies on one side or the other. I chose it because it is an excellent example of an intelligent person trained in one field arguing with experts in another field. Such challenges are not, of course, always successful; the expert may have replies which are decisive. But sometimes such a challenge may reveal basic assumptions which are unsupported or gaps in reasoning.

To choose another example, suppose we have what purports to be an eyewitness account of a fifteenth-century battle, written in an old manuscript. Science may be able to tell us whether the paper, ink, style of handwriting, etc., are as old as the fifteenth century. But if they are not, this does not prove the document a forgery. Old documents can be recopied, and often were when paper was less durable than modern paper. We must use our historical knowledge and our estimate of the plausibility and convincingness of the account given of the battle to decide whether we have an eyewitness account.

I am not, in these examples, trying to discredit science. Rather, I am arguing that in many cases science can only provide data, which must be combined with our own reasoning, experience, and common sense for us to reach conclusions. To let our mind be made up for us by a survey or a study or a group of figures is often unreasonable.

This is true when values are involved. Medical science can tell you the relation between smoking and lung cancer. Only you can decide how these figures should affect your own behavior. A survey can tell you that a given teacher's courses are unpopular, but your own experience may tell you that you have learned a great deal from him. Science gives us a tremendous body of organized information about the universe, but our own reasoning must measure whatever philosophical or religious conclusions are drawn from this information.

I conclude this book by reminding you that logic has its limitations. Logic is not a substitute for observation and experiment in acquiring factual information. It is not a substitute for our own experience in discovering our own likes and dislikes, strengths and weaknesses. No one ever fell in love because he thought it was the logical thing to do. Acts of sanctity or heroism rise above logic, as emotions, tastes and whims fall below it. Life is larger than logic. But to abandon reason and logic, which is the science and art of reasoning, is to become less than human. Socrates, whose questioning and arguing were the origin of philosophy in the West, said that the unthinking life was not worth living. Many of us try to live our lives without thinking. Whether we shall find such lives in the long run worth living is another question.

CASES

1. Go through current magazines and newspapers looking for uses of *scientific* and related terms. What seems to be meant by the term in each of these uses? Has the hypothetico-deductive method actually been used? Is there any evidence of a Positivistic sense of *scientific* in any of your examples?

Formulate a null and alternative hypothesis for each of the following. Indicate what you would expect to observe if the null hypothesis were true and what you would expect to observe if the alternative hypothesis were true. So far as you know, which hypothesis should be accepted? Why? Devise an experiment for each case.

2. Effect of marijuana use on study habits.
3. Relative intelligence of conservative and radical college students.
4. Relative attractiveness of members and nonmembers of Women's Liberation groups.
5. Effects of improved living conditions on militancy of minority-group members.
6. Relation of intelligence to religious belief.
7. Discuss at least one questionable position or theory that claims scientific backing. What is the source of your doubts? How might a supporter of the position or theory reply to your doubts? How could the issue be settled?

SUGGESTED READING

In this bibliography I list books that will take you one or two steps further in some of the topics that we have been considering.

If you want to acquire further expertise in logic, perhaps even to become a logician or philosopher, you may want to read:

Purtill, R. L.: *Logic for Philosophers*, Harper & Row, New York, 1971.

If the history of logic interests you, this book is the best modern history:

Kneale, W. and Kneale, M.: *The Development of Logic*, Oxford University Press, New York, 1954.

The history of fallacies and a careful examination of the weaknesses of many modern treatments of them can be found in:

Hamblin, C. L.: *Fallacies*, Methuen, London, 1970.

An enjoyable treatment of the logic of syllogisms with many delightful examples is provided by the author of *Alice in Wonderland:*

Carroll, L.: *Symbolic Logic and the Game of Logic*, Dover, New York, 1958.

This book is one of the best detailed discussions of scientific method:

Wilson, E. B.: *An Introduction to Scientific Research*, McGraw-Hill, New York, 1952.

An excellent treatment of logical thinking in relation to reading and writing, with many good examples, is:

Altick, R. D.: *Preface to Critical Reading*, Holt, Rinehart and Winston, New York, 1967.

Finally, here is an application of logical thinking to important philosophical problems:

Wheatley, J.: *Prolegomenon to Philosophy*, Wadsworth, Belmont, California, 1970.

INDEX